To my parents, Ken and Marlene Schrager,
who recognized early on that being
different is sometimes better.

FRIED & TRUE

MORE THAN 50 RECIPES *for*
AMERICA'S BEST
FRIED CHICKEN *and* SIDES

Foreword by Whoopi Goldberg
Photographs by Evan Sung

LEE BRIAN SCHRAGER

with **ADEENA SUSSMAN**

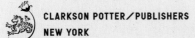

CLARKSON POTTER/PUBLISHERS
NEW YORK

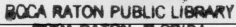

Copyright © 2014 by Lee Brian Schrager
Photographs copyright © 2014 by Evan Sung

Published in the United States by Clarkson Potter/
Publishers, an imprint of the Crown Publishing Group,
a division of Random House LLC, a Penguin Random
House Company, New York.
www.crownpublishing.com
www.clarksonpotter.com

CLARKSON POTTER is a trademark and POTTER with
colophon is a registered trademark of Random House LLC.

Permission acknowledgments can be found on page 256.

Library of Congress Cataloging-in-Publication Data
Schrager, Lee.
   Fried & true : more than 50 recipes for America's best
fried chicken and sides / Lee Brian Schrager with Adeena
Sussman ; photographs by Evan Sung. — First edition.
      pages cm
   Includes index.
   1. Cooking (Chicken) 2. Fried food. 3. Side dishes
(Cooking) 4. Cooking, American—Southern style. 5.
Schrager, Lee—Travel—Southern States. 6. Restaurants—
Southern States. I. Sussman, Adeena. II. Title. III. Title:
Fried and true.
   TX750.5.C45S37 2014
   641.5975—dc23
                                        2013050631

ISBN 978-0-7704-3522-6
eBook ISBN 978-0-7704-3523-3

Printed in the United States

Text design by Danielle Deschenes
Cover design by Danielle Deschenes
Cover photography by Evan Sung

10 9 8 7 6 5 4 3 2 1

First Edition

CONTENTS

FOREWORD

by Whoopi Goldberg

WHO DOESN'T DIG FRIED CHICKEN? If you're a vegan you probably don't, and in that case put this book down, 'coz you're not going to be able to resist the desire for that chicken. Fried chicken is a staple in many cultures. It's comfort food, and it isn't a black, Asian, or white Southern thing—it's a human thing. I LOVE my fried chicken. I mean I really, really, really, really LOVE my fried chicken. Nothing makes me or my mouth happier. I remember my mom taking the brown paper bag, adding the flour, putting in the chicken and shaking, shaking, shaking. And when it hit the oil . . . that smell! I'm not much of a cook myself, but I do know my fried chicken. (I cook a mean turkey once a year at Thanksgiving; really slow, all night, and baste, baste, baste). But fried chicken is my one true love.

Each year there is something called the Food Network South Beach and New York City Wine & Food Festivals. A few years ago, the very amazing Rachael Ray couldn't make it to her event, the Burger Bash. The most generous man, Lee Schrager, approached me to fill in. Now, who doesn't like a great burger? So that was an easy "yes" for me! But as I was walking from station to station sampling all the burgers from everywhere, I turned to Lee and suggested a fried chicken event for the following year. I'm proud to be part of Chicken Coupe, now going into its fourth year in New York and its third year in Miami. (Thanks, Lee!) But who knew Lee was such a fried chicken fan, too? He says writing a fried chicken cookbook wasn't always on his bucket list . . . but now I'm not so sure.

Fried & True doesn't just give you 50-plus fried chicken recipes—from the ones Lee picked up on his road trip to some from the best restaurants, in some of the best cities in the world—but also the stories that go along with them and make for some good reading. My favorite is "Fried Chicken 101"—yup, tips! Um-hm . . . "don't crowd, and give each piece time." That's good advice.

Thanks, Lee—I'm hoping to meet some of these recipes at the next Chicken Coupe event.

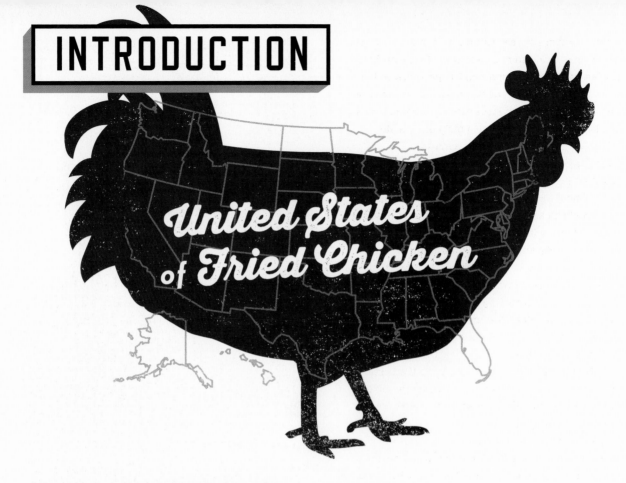

United States of Fried Chicken

MY EARLIEST CHILDHOOD FOOD MEMORIES revolve around fried chicken, my adult food obsession. Growing up on Long Island in the town of Massapequa, I always looked forward to my mother's best homemade dish: fried chicken, which she prepared in her burnt-orange Le Creuset Dutch oven to much approval from my father, my two brothers, and myself. On Saturday evenings, when my parents would head out for date night, they'd order dinner to be delivered from our favorite restaurant, Chicken Delight. I can still see the beat-up red Volkswagen delivery vehicle, with a smiling plastic bird perched on the roof, pulling into our driveway on Beverly Road. As it arrived, the bird would seem to chirp: "Don't cook tonight, call Chicken Delight!" Nowadays I can't seem to remember where I ate dinner the week before, but even more than forty years later, those two off-white cardboard plates, stapled together to form a covered dish, are crystal clear in my mind's eye. Inside was a full quarter of miraculously hot fried chicken, the longest, tastiest fries known to mankind, and a Parker House roll that absorbed the chicken's delicious grease. I'm also incredibly nostalgic for the all-you-can-eat fried chicken buffet at Howard Johnson's. Held underneath the restaurant's iconic orange rooftop, the buffet included mountains of fried chicken, creamy coleslaw, and as many fries as you could eat.

It was a sad day indeed when my friends and I were politely asked not to return to that HoJo's on Sunrise Boulevard; we had surpassed the per-person limit at an all-you-can-eat buffet. To this day, it's nearly impossible for me to resist ordering a plate of fried chicken, whether it be from a strip mall, white-tablecloth restaurant, Korean restaurant, or a take-out joint I pass while driving on the highway. I'm proud to say that these days I usually skip the fries and soda, but I almost never leave the biscuit untouched.

Fried chicken has a long storied, and much beloved history in this country. It is believed that Scottish immigrants originally brought the dish to the United States in the 1700s. West African slaves added their own spices and techniques, perfecting the dish in both their masters' kitchens and their own; some even sold poultry and made fried chicken in their spare time to sell for extra income. From that original tradition the dish traveled across the country, and in the past decade or so it's begun to rival other American mainstays—burgers, pizza, barbecue—in popularity. And as we speak, fried chicken is clearly having a moment—everywhere you look, restaurants are perfecting an authentic Southern version, or lending their own touches and ethnic influences. When the idea for a whole book on the subject came to me a couple of years back, this "it" food was still gathering steam. When I added a fried chicken event, aptly named FRIED and now in its third year as Chicken Coupe, to the Food Network New York City Wine & Food Festival, I had no idea what I'd be starting. Our nation's great chefs, secret frybird lovers at heart, have had a lot to do with it, researching and experimenting and elevating the dish in ways you may not see—but can certainly taste.

Writing this book also brought low-key fried chicken lovers out of the woodwork. When we photographed these dishes during a long, hot summer week in New York City, a never-ending line of friends, family—and even building employees—formed to sample our on-set batches, debating their favorites with us each day as skillets of oil bubbled

in the kitchen. Which was the best? Was it Atlanta chef Asha Gomez's Indian-inspired fried chicken and waffles? The classic chicken-and-biscuits combo from Scott Peacock? Or maybe it was Yotam Ottolenghi's seeded chicken schnitzel. And who could forget Art Smith's fried chicken with Swiss chard and pine nuts, Michelle Bernstein's version with a side of watermelon Greek salad, or the pale, yet flavor-packed, gluten-free version from Ina's in Chicago? The debate rages on.

Before this book, I had only prepared fried chicken once. Even after graduating from culinary school and working for great restaurants and for prestigious caterers along the way, it was not an everyday dish for me. Back in the 1980s, while attending Florida International University during the day, I worked the graveyard shift as a short-order cook at Broward General Medical Center. One of my standard orders to fulfill was a four-piece of Tyson fried chicken, a portion-controlled package I learned to drop into the deep-fry basket for exactly twelve minutes. This was a shortcut recipe, designed to get customers fed and happy and out the door. And now I've rediscovered that while fried chicken can be a glorious multiple-day affair, it can also be as simple as cooking gets: cut up chicken, dip in buttermilk, dredge in seasoned flour, and fry until golden brown. That's why at the end of the day this classic has staying power, not only in the South—where it's still the centerpiece of countless Sunday suppers—but all around the country, where people just can't get enough of it.

One of the best parts of working on this book was a road trip we took to three fried chicken strongholds: New Orleans, Atlanta, and Nashville. In addition to sampling amazing food in each city, the pocket trivia and stories we picked up along the way were incredible. The most inspiring part of our journey was the opportunity to make some amazing new friends and learn life lessons from them. True wisdom comes from experience, and few have more than Leah Chase of Dooky Chase's in New Orleans's Treme neighborhood (for her full story, see page 83). "We changed the course of America over a bowl of gumbo," Mrs. Chase told me, but I believe her trays of fried chicken had just as much to do with it.

By no means did we ever hope to capture every great fried chicken recipe for our book (and greatness in this category is highly subjective). We don't cover every state or every well-known place in the country—that would have been impossible. And many storied places had recipes we knew we'd never be able to get—and wouldn't deign to try to re-create; some traditions are best left alone. What we hoped to do was share some of our favorites, using the recipes to tell the story of a treasured dish and its many varieties. You'll see many twists, from Mediterranean and Asian to Cuban, Israeli, and West African. All can be eaten in the United States. All have become part of our culinary canon. And *all* of them are amazingly delicious.

There are many things that I hoped to do in my lifetime, but writing a book about fried chicken wasn't on my original "bucket list." Now that it's done, I can tell you that it was one of the most exciting, delicious, and humbling experiences of my career to date. I hope you enjoy this book as much as the "cluck team" has enjoyed traveling, testing, and tasting together to bring it to you.

Lee Brian Schrager

FRIED CHICKEN 101

Making fried chicken isn't as hard as it may seem; it just takes preparation and organization. Like any other kitchen endeavor worth undertaking, it's about having the right tools, picking the right ingredients, and knowing a few tips and tricks that will have you frying like a pro in no time. But before you get started, first consider these suggestions, so you have the basic principles of the freedom to fry in mind:

BE PREPARED: An organized kitchen and a game plan are a fryer's best friends. Everything will go more smoothly if you read each recipe from start to finish and prepare all of the elements—brine, dredge, seasoning, oil—in advance, making sure everything's ready before you start.

CLEAR THE FRIDGE: For recipes that require brining or marinating, clear the proper amount of shelf space and adjust shelf height in your fridge for whatever vessel you are using. This will eliminate panicked, last-minute rearranging.

BRINING: Brining may seem like a labor-intensive extra step, but it really does add a whole 'nother layer of goodness to the finished product. Like most foods, chicken benefits from a healthy dose of sodium, which ups the flavor considerably. Typically the number one ingredient in brines (other than water), salt performs double duty, both tenderizing the meat by breaking down its cellular structure *and* helping enhance the tastiness of the chicken itself. Brines can range from two hours to two days and can also contain sugar, buttermilk, herbs, and spices. That being said, if you like the look of a recipe but don't have time for brining, don't sweat it—your chicken will still be delish.

> **NOTE:** *Don't have time to brine? Buy a kosher chicken. The primary ingredient in most brines is salt, and kosher chickens are presalted. They'll help you achieve the salty, moist juiciness that is the hallmark of a brined bird.*

SEASONINGS: Incorporating a variety of herbs, spices, and seasonings is one way to really make this process your own. Smoked paprika, turmeric, cardamom, sesame seeds—the sky (or the fry) is the limit. While many recipes call for a precise formula, we won't tell if you pinch and guesstimate your way to the finish line. Onion powder and garlic powder are ubiquitous for the mellow, earthy warmth they bring to the table. Black and white peppers and chili powder lend a subtle, irreplaceable edge, while sweet paprika provides a grounded sweetness. Dried herbs like oregano, thyme—even rosemary—contribute hints of grassy garden freshness.

CHILL FOR THE "SHRINK-WRAP" EFFECT: As we tested the recipes for this book, we noticed that many cooks—most notably those from New Orleans—specified using well-chilled chicken for frying, believing that it promotes a crispier crust. While our results aren't scientific, we did notice that using a cold bird helps coating adhere to the chicken's skin, resulting in skin that shrinks and practically becomes one with the bird beneath.

FLOUR POWER AND THE DOUBLE DIP: In recipes that call for dredging the chicken, some use what may seem like an excessive amount of flour. Fret not: some chefs feel that tossing the chicken lightly in a larger amount of flour dredge helps promote a lighter, flakier finished product. Some people love a thick, crunchy crust above all else, and with recipes consisting of passing chicken through both wet and dry mixtures, you can easily achieve it by double-dipping in both wet and dry components.

DEEP FRYING: While most chefs agree that a cast-iron skillet is the frying pan of choice, many do turn to deep frying, which has several advantages—primarily, that a large pot filled halfway with oil generally splatters less, creating less mess, and that since the oil surrounds all parts of the chicken at once, deep-fried chicken cooks faster than skillet-fried. No flipping required.

COUNTERTOP DEEP FRYERS: If you're only frying a few pieces, or have the time to do several batches, a good-quality countertop deep fryer can have some advantages. One, you'll be able to regulate your oil temperature with ease. Two, the closed environment helps contain odors and splatters. And three, hot oil has a cosseted environment in which to safely cool down.

SKILLET FRYING: For the true Southern experience, nothing beats frying in a cast-iron skillet, which cooks chicken evenly and helps develop a crispy, perfectly burnished crust. Many cooks have a collection of skillets, some passed down from generation to generation, and some, like Charles Gabriel (see page 52) custom-order giant versions. To start your own collection, buy a new or vintage Lodge brand 12-inch skillet.

USE A THERMOMETER: Though you don't need one, a deep-fry or candy thermometer will make this process much easier. You'll know exactly when your oil is ready for frying and be able to easily adjust the heat as needed as the oil temperature rises and falls. Both old-fashioned mercury and newfangled digital models do the trick.

KEEP IT HOT: Nothing's sadder than a soggy batch of fried chicken, and the culprit is usually oil whose temperature has sunk too low. To avoid this pitfall, make sure your oil is properly heated before adding your chicken and between batches, and use your deep-fry thermometer to monitor the highs and lows of frying.

> **NOTE:** *When you first add the chicken to hot oil, the oil temperature will drop. You may need to raise the heat to bring the oil back up to ideal frying temperature, so keep an eye on that thermometer.*

DON'T CROWD: Though the temptation to fry more pieces at once gets the best of us, crowding your deep-frying or skillet environment can lead to uneven cooking and longer-than-necessary frying times.

GIVE EACH PIECE TIME: Different pieces of the bird take different amounts of time to cook. Note that when frying a mix of breasts, wings, and thighs, the smaller pieces will cook faster than the breasts, so watch for the ideal color of crust and check the internal temperature to be sure each piece is done.

HEAVEN SCENT: If there's one thing that prevents people from frying chicken at home, it's the lingering scent of frying that seems to cling to every nook and cranny. Though a cross-ventilated kitchen or a vented hood helps mitigate the situation, we've found that the best solution is a simmering pot of warm spices. Fill a saucepan halfway with water and add your favorite whole spices: cinnamon sticks, star anise, allspice berries, cloves. Powdered spices work, too, but the whole ones keep on giving all day. Just make sure to watch the water level, continuing to fill the saucepan when the water has evaporated.

DISCARD SAFELY: Once you're finished with your oil and ready to discard it, cool it completely and pour it carefully into a shatter-proof container with a tight-fitting lid. You can throw it away with the rest of your trash, or seek out a location in your area that recycles cooking oil for biodiesel (Google in your area for the closest location; some will even pick up for free).

Part I: TOOLS FOR FRYING AT HOME

Great news: assembling your fried chicken toolkit will be a breeze, since the majority of items are probably in your kitchen drawers right now. Knowing how to use them will make frying chicken not only a safe, easy process—but a fun one.

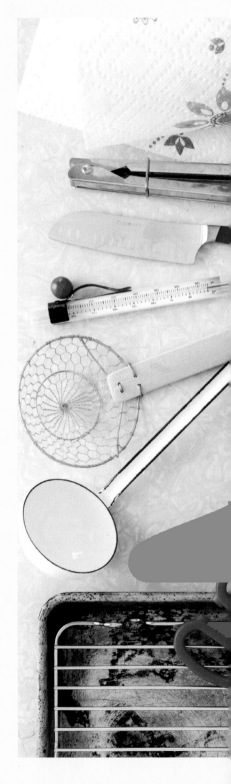

❑ **DEEP-FRY OR CANDY THERMOMETER:** Since temperature is key, a thermometer is essential to proper deep-frying. Look for one with an adjustable clip, which will allow you to secure the thermometer to a variety of frying vessels. If you plan on skillet-frying, a smaller model will do; for deep-frying in a large pot, seek out a taller model, either digital or mercury.

❑ **MEAT THERMOMETER:** This inexpensive gadget will help you gauge the internal temperature of fried chicken, ensuring perfect doneness every time.

❑ **CHINESE SPIDER:** For easily lowering chicken into a deep-fryer and then removing it when cooked, nothing gets the job done like this inexpensive implement with roots in the Chinese kitchen. Whereas a slotted spoon might trap oil, a spider's gridlike wire construction siphons every last drop of extraneous fat away from the chicken.

❑ **POULTRY SHEARS:** To easily break down whole chickens, invest in a good pair of poultry shears, which makes butchering your bird a breeze. Look for a set with easy-grip handles and easily disassembled parts— you'll want to take them apart for easy cleaning.

❑ **TONGS:** Use tongs to rotate the chicken in a cast-iron skillet as you fry. Though they come in many different lengths, 8- or 10-inch models are long enough to prevent splatter burns, yet short enough to give you maximum maneuverability.

❑ **LADLE AND SAUCEPAN:** To prevent hot-oil messes while deep-frying, keep a small ladle and empty saucepan near the stove. If, while lowering your chicken into the pot or deep-fryer, you find that bubbling oil is precipitously close to overflowing, simply transfer a few ladlefuls of oil to the empty saucepan (this oil can be used for other batches of chicken).

❑ **CAST-IRON SKILLET:** The heart and soul of pan-fried chicken, your cast-iron skillet will become a source of passion and pride. They are shockingly inexpensive, and their solid-state construction helps promote even cooking and eliminate "hot spots" on your range. Though you'll want to invest in a range of sizes, a 10- or 12-inch Lodge brand skillet is perfect for frying up a whole bird. Some recipes call for a skillet with a tight-fitting lid; if you don't have a matching one, do your best by mixing and matching from your home collection.

> **NOTE:** *To easily clean a skillet, do not—and we repeat, DO NOT— run it through the dishwasher or even wash thoroughly with hot water and soap. Instead, wipe out any extra oil and loose bits with a soft kitchen towel, then add several tablespoons of kosher salt to the pan and move the salt around with the towel; the salt will help lift any bits stuck to the bottom of the skillet. Then, using a cloth or a paper towel, wipe the inside of the skillet with a thin slick of neutral-flavored oil.*

❑ **WIRE RACK AND RIMMED BAKING SHEET:** An airy rack with plenty of space between rows or grids will allow extra oil to drain away from freshly fried chicken; a rimmed baking sheet set underneath prevents drips from getting messy. Look for both in the baking section of the kitchen-supply store or larger supermarkets.

❑ **PAPER TOWELS:** If you don't have a wire rack for draining just-fried chicken, paper towels get the job done just fine—line a plate with a few sheets, put your finished chicken pieces on top, and sprinkle with salt as directed. Use paper towels to clean up oil splatters around the stove—and to wrap a drumstick tip before snacking.

❑ **SHARP KNIFE:** Use for trimming extra fat from chicken pieces, or for breaking down larger breast pieces in two. (When separating a chicken into pieces, always cut between joints if possible, rather than through them—it will be easier on you and on your knife.)

❑ **LARGE, DEEP POT OR DUTCH OVEN:** Many chefs and cooks enjoy deep-frying, which yields evenly browned chicken with less hands-on maintenance. For such recipes, we prefer a plain old stockpot or Dutch oven. Use a heavy-bottomed 6- or 8-quart pot.

Part II: OILS AND FATS

The recipes in this book call for an incredible variety of oils and fats, each with their own attributes and taste distinctions. Though there's often a reason for the specific choices, feel free to mix and match based on your preference—and based on what you have in your pantry.

Oil's temperature drops precipitously with every piece of chicken you add to your skillet or pot, often taking several minutes to return to its desired temperature range. One trick we've learned: when deep-frying, heat your oil 20 to 25 degrees above the desired frying temperature. That way, the recovery time back to the optimal temperature will be minimal. But keep in mind that the so-called *smoke point* of oil is the point at which it begins to burn and develop acrid flavor; when frying, watch your thermometer to make sure to control your oil before it reaches the point of no return; once it's smokin', it's toast.

> **NOTE:** *Oil is expensive, so good news: if you maintain the proper frying temperature, yes, you can reuse frying oil. After frying a first batch of chicken, cool the oil completely, then strain it through a coffee filter into a container with an airtight lid. Cover tightly and store in a cool place. This process can be repeated through one or two more uses, at which point the oil should be discarded. Frying oil should only work to crisp the bird efficiently or, in the case of the addition of lard or bacon, lend subtle flavor that enhances the chicken itself. If you're tasting the oil rather than the chicken, it's time to introduce a fresh batch.*

1 BACON GREASE: The next time you fry up a batch of bacon for breakfast, hold on to that fat! Adding a few splashes of rendered bacon fat to a larger amount of frying oil makes for pleasingly smoky poultry. The smoke point isn't as important here, as it's going to constitute only a small portion of the total amount of oil.

2 CANOLA OIL: *Smoke point: 400°F.* Neutral in flavor, with a stable frying temperature, canola is a reliable choice for deep fryers and large pots of oil (relatively speaking, it's also the most cost-effective). Reuse two to three times, cooling and straining between uses, before discarding. Other similar oils to consider: safflower, sunflower, vegetable.

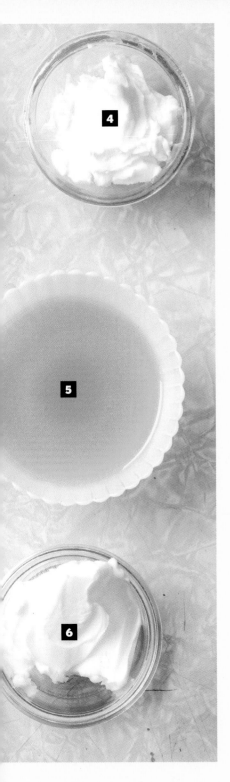

3 **UNSALTED BUTTER:** *Smoke point: 350°F.* Be inspired by the classic Southern recipe revived and made famous by Edna Lewis, and consider adding a little butter into the frying-oil mix. The creamy, rich touch of dairy only enhances the indulgence factor of any fried chicken preparation. If you have the time, quickly clarify the butter by simmering it, then discarding the foam that gathers on the top as well as the whey that sinks to the bottom. This significantly raises the butter's smoke point, enabling you to fry freely.

4 **VEGETABLE SHORTENING:** *Smoke point: 370°F.* Shelf-stable vegetable shortening, often made from cottonseed oil, melts down quickly from its solid form and can be a handy backup to keep in your pantry. As is the case when used in pie crusts, vegetable shortening encourages flakiness and adds levity to the proceedings. Since it's partially hydrogenated—a chemical process that transforms oil from liquid to solid form—and technically contains traces of trans fat, it's a somewhat controversial choice. But we're not here to judge—just to give you all the options.

5 **CORN OIL:** *Smoke point: 375°F.* A popular Southern choice, corn oil is an underappreciated frying fat that imparts well-rounded, slightly buttery notes to the finished product. Make sure to seek out a refined oil (as most corn oils are) whose smoke point makes it suitable for frying.

6 **LARD:** *Smoke point: 370°F.* The new wave of Southern chefs loves blending lard into fried chicken recipes. Its porky goodness ties the recipe back to its down-home roots and makes for an extra-light, flaky crust. Though you can find shelf-stable lard in most supermarkets, it may have been bleached or rehydrogenated, and its flavor funkiness is an acquired taste. For mellower, top-quality—yet still sufficiently piggy—lard, seek out leaf lard. Rendered from the area surrounding a pig's kidney, pure rendered leaf lard is snowy white, creamy, and a truly original choice. Unrendered leaf lard can be purchased from www.flyingpigsfarm.com, but you have to render it yourself; for utter convenience and top quality, you can order rendered leaf lard in varying sized tubs from www.prairiepridepork.com in Minnesota. Costly, but worth every penny.

PEANUT OIL: *Smoke point: 440°F.* A favorite of Southern cooks, peanut oil imparts a subtle nuttiness as well as a dark, burnished shade to a properly fried crust. Remember to ask any potential eaters if they've got a peanut allergy!

Part III: HOW TO CUT UP A CHICKEN

If there's one thing almost universally agreed upon, it's that butchering a bird at home is far superior to buying one that's been precut. Not only can you assess the quality of the entire chicken for yourself and determine when it was butchered, but you won't get stuck paying by weight for all that extra skin hidden underneath the plastic wrapping. Tom Stone, of famed chicken purveyor Bell & Evans, notes that by butchering the bird yourself, you'll also avoid losing valuable juice that begins to escape the chicken the second it's cut. Once you get the hang of it, using the natural series of "fat lines" that divide the chicken as your guide, you can cut up an entire chicken in a matter of minutes.

1 **REMOVE THE LEG QUARTERS:** Place the chicken on a clean cutting board. Using a sharp knife, gently cut a small slit through the skin connecting the breast to the thigh; apply pressure underneath to expose the thigh bone. Cut through the joint to remove the leg; repeat with the other side of the chicken.

2 **DIVIDE THE LEG QUARTERS:** Place a leg quarter skin side down. Expose the thin line of fat that covers the joint separating the drumstick from the thigh. Cut straight through this line to separate the drumstick from the thigh. Repeat with the other leg quarter.

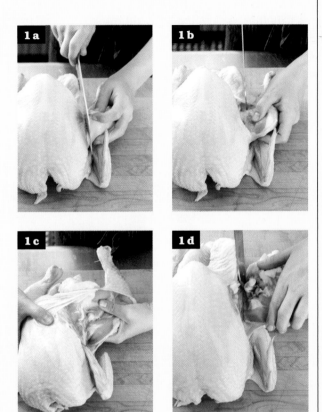

3 REMOVE THE WINGS FROM THE BREASTS: With the whole breast portion resting on the cutting board, lift it up by one of the wings, pulling the wings away and upward and using your thumb to expose the joint separating the wing from the breast. Cut around the joint to separate the wing from the breast; repeat on the other side.

4 REMOVE THE BACK: Identify the fat lines that separate the ribs from the breasts. Using poultry or kitchen shears, cut through the ribs to remove the backbone (you can either reserve it for making stock, or batter and fry it as a "bonus piece").

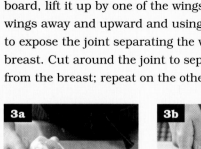

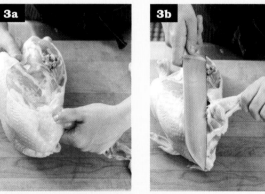

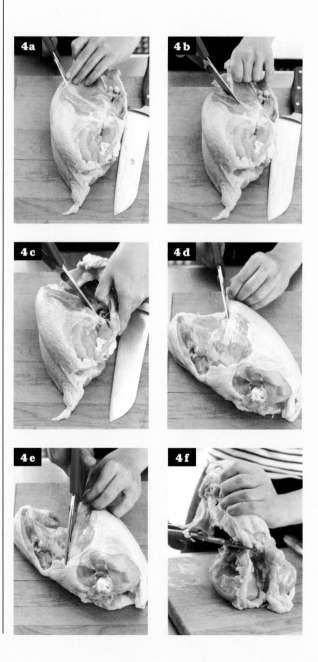

5 REMOVE THE KEEL BONE: With the breast side on the cutting board, make a slit through the blade-shaped cartilage tip at the top of the breast. Bend the breast back to loosen the keel bone. Use your fingers to feel underneath the cartilage and pop out and discard the keel bone. Using the heels of your hands, gently press down to flatten the breasts.

6 SEPARATE THE BREASTS: Using your knife, divide the breast into two equal-sized portions. For recipes calling for ten pieces of chicken, divide each breast half into two pieces.

5a

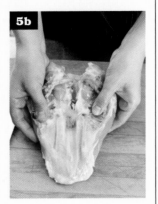

5b

6a

6b

5c

6c

6d

If you select a whole chicken from the super-market aisle, take it to the meat counter: most butchers will cut up the chicken for you free of charge. Then you're free to take it home and fry, fry away.

Part IV: **CHOOSING YOUR CHICKEN**

Like any artisan food, fried chicken is only as good as the sum of its parts. In this case, the most important part is the chicken itself. Don't get us wrong—one of the best things about fried chicken is that it's easy and relatively inexpensive. Chicken, salt, spices, flour, buttermilk—and you're in business. If there's one place you're going to splurge, it should be on the bird itself. Seek out quality birds at your local farmers' market, specialty store, or supermarket. Look for smaller chickens, ones weighing somewhere between 2½ and 3½ pounds. (Unless otherwise specified, we've chosen a 3- to 3½-pound bird for each recipe.) This weight indicates a younger chicken, which translates into tender flesh, unfettered flavor, and pieces that cook up just a little bit faster. Look for chickens labeled "fryer" or "broiler," usually under 2 months old and within the optimal weight range, says Tom Stone of Bell & Evans. "Roasters" are older chickens and can weigh anywhere between 3½ and 5 pounds; though smaller is better, they work fine, too.

When purchasing your poultry, seek out air-chilled chicken. By law chickens must be kept cold once butchered, a benchmark most major companies achieve by submerging the chicken in chlorinated water. This process tends to dissolve some of the chicken's flavorful fat and artificially plumps the chicken, passing along the water weight to the consumer. That liquid also escapes faster than natural moisture during cooking, so look for chicken that has been air-chilled. Also look for chickens that have been fed a vegetable-based, hormone- and antibiotic-free diet, which results in chicken with cleaner flavor.

SOUTHERN INSPIRATIONS

IF ONE AMERICAN REGION can claim fried chicken as its own, it's the South. More than in any other part of the country, Southern chefs and cooks told us tales of Sunday suppers, pre- and post-church repasts, family reunions, and other festive meals where fried chicken played a pivotal role in the proceedings. It makes sense, when you think about it: particularly where hot weather prevails, fried chicken can be made early in the morning, then covered with a tea towel and served at room temperature with all the fixings. It is cost-effective and can feed a crowd. Most important, everyone loves it—and we're quite sure you will, too. Though there are as many permutations on fried chicken in the South as elsewhere, a few themes prevail. Several recipes use lard as part of the frying oil; many are dipped in buttermilk, then dredged in seasoned flour; and the use of a cast-iron skillet often defines a recipe as hailing from below the Mason-Dixon line.

OPPOSITE: Arnold's Country Kitchen's Fried Chicken, Chicken Livers, Braised Turnip Greens, and Fried Green Tomatoes, see page 38 for recipe.

16
CHICAGO, IL

3
SAN FRANCISCO, CA

11
YOUNTVILLE, CA

7 **8** **9** **12**
NEW ORLEANS, LA

LAKE PLACID, NY `17`

HARLEM, NY `4`

NEW YORK, NY `10` `18`

ASHEVILLE, NC `15`

CHARLESTON, SC `20`

ATLANTA, GA `6` `13` `14`

SAVANNAH, GA `19`

NASHVILLE, TN `1` `2` `5`

MIAMI, FL `18`

1 ARNOLD'S COUNTRY KITCHEN *Fried Chicken, Chicken Livers, Braised Turnip Greens, and Fried Green Tomatoes*

2 HATTIE B'S *Hot Chicken*

3 TYLER FLORENCE *Fried Chicken and Velvety Mashed Potatoes*

4 CHARLES GABRIEL *Country Pan-Fried Chicken and Candied Yams*

5 THE LOVELESS CAFÉ *Fried Chicken and Hash Brown Casserole*

6 LINTON HOPKINS *"Naked" Fried Chicken and Old-Fashioned Coleslaw*

7 JACQUES LEONARDI *Jacques-Imo's Fried Chicken and Smothered Cabbage*

8 DONALD LINK *Sunday Night Fried Chicken and Lake Charles Dirty Rice*

9 KERMIT RUFFINS AND RAY "BOOM BOOM" *Hard-Fried Chicken*

10 ELIZABETH KARMEL *Hill Country Buttermilk Fried Chicken, Cheese Grits, and Candied Country Ham*

11 THOMAS KELLER *Buttermilk Fried Chicken*

12 VENESSA WILLIAMS *Cajun Moon Funky Fried Chicken and New Orleans–Style Vegetarian Red Beans and Rice*

13 MARY MAC'S TEA ROOM *Fried Chicken and Tomato Pie*

14 SCOTT PEACOCK *Edna's Fried Chicken and Classic Buttermilk Biscuits*

15 SEVEN SOWS *Fried Chicken with Egg and Giblet Gravy, and Macaroni and Cheese*

16 ART SMITH *Fried Chicken and Swiss Chard Salad with Pine Nuts and Lemon*

17 JACQUES PÉPIN *Fried Chicken Southern-Style with Corn Bread Sticks*

18 ANDREW CARMELLINI *The Dutch's Fried Chicken*

19 PAULA DEEN *Best Ever Southern Fried Chicken*

20 MARTHA LOU GADSDEN *Martha Lou's Fried Chicken*

Arnold's, Prince's, and Bolton's Hot Chicken

WE'D HEARD SO MUCH ABOUT NASHVILLE'S HOT CHICKEN, we half expected our eyes to shed cayenne tears the minute we hit the tarmac on a steamy June morning. But it was early, so before we headed over for our first sampling of the city's hyperregional fried chicken specialty, we paid a visit to Arnold's Country Kitchen to experience so-called "meat-and-three," traditionally a joint serving a protein with three side dishes.

Part of Arnold's charm is its democratic system of ordering; whether you're a county judge or a biker with a ZZ Top–style beard, you don't get your food until you put in your time on the cafeteria-style line. The walls display pictures of just a fraction of the famous fans who've come through—Merle Haggard, Pam Tillis, Hayden Panettiere, and Kelly Clarkson, to name a few—not to mention a shout-out from the patron saint of Southern cooking preservation himself, John T. Edge, and his Southern Foodways Alliance. The fried chicken and sides were incredible (see the recipes on page 38), but as in any great establishment, the food is only as good as the people who make it—and the Arnold family charmed the pants off us. Jack stays home most of the time these days, but his wife, Rosario, stands behind the counter radiating genuine Southern charm combined with a touch of Latin fire, courtesy of her native Colombia. Their three sons—Mon, 37; Khalil, 36; and Franz, 24—run the business with her, and it's gratifying to witness the expression of an unspoken contract that all but guarantees the boys will be ushering Arnold's into the next generation. We said our good-byes, feeling like we'd become part of the Arnold family, but knew it was time to head on to Prince's Hot Chicken.

OPPOSITE, CLOCKWISE FROM TOP: The line outside Arnold's Country Kitchen; Khalil Arnold, hard at work; outside Prince's Hot Chicken Shack; finished plates at Arnold's

Prince's Hot Chicken Shack

ABOVE: Andre Prince Jeffries (at right) and her daughter Semone Jeffries

OPPOSITE: Selling chess pie by the slice at the register at Prince's

Located in a strip mall, Prince's is a modest establishment whose historical significance far eclipses its surroundings. As we sat at one of the worn wooden tables and waited for owner Andre Prince Jeffries, women sold individually wrapped slices of chess pie to a steady stream of customers near the register. Everyone waved to Andre when she finally walked in, lugging a well-worn shopping bag silk-screened with a rooster. A mere few weeks after the James Beard Foundation had bestowed Prince's with an "American Classics" award in New York, Andre seemed still to be glowing. We were all melting from the heat, but Andre, nary a bead of sweat on her brow, began to tell us the story of her great-uncle, Thornton Prince, who founded Prince's. "He *was* good-looking," said Andre of Thornton. "And a womanizer, which, if I admit it, runs in the Prince family." Legend has it that Thornton's girl-

friend, indignant at his indiscretions, harvested the hottest peppers she could find from her garden and squeezed their invisibly incendiary juice on a plate of his fried chicken. Thornton survived, got hooked on the idea of a hot chicken shack, and opened the original Prince's downtown. Eventually Prince's moved to its current location, and the business passed through the hands of several relatives, but Andre stuck with it. "My goal was to keep it in the family and the heritage," said Andre. "I had no idea I'd be in here myself thirty-four years later."

Though she has managed to keep the chicken's formula—which comes mild, medium, hot, or extra hot—a well-guarded secret, pretty much everyone agrees that the two principal ingredients are lard and cayenne, combined in mysterious proportions and brushed on the chicken just out of the fryer, lacquering it a shocking shade of red (see the recipe on page 45 from our friends at Hattie B's, who jerry-rigged a home version for us). Sinus-clearing, Scoville-busting, twelve-alarm—there are no descriptors to properly describe the experience of biting into a piece of Prince's. Based on decades of informal research, Andre had decided that women can tolerate extra hot better than men, chalking it up to the experience of labor pains. "One of my male customers says he eats his in a bathtub filled with ice-cold water," she told us. So protective is Andre of her extra hot spice blend that she shuttles it to and from the restaurant in that aforementioned, fowl-emblazoned shopping bag, protecting her precious currency. "I don't want anyone overusing it," she said. "And besides, it can be dangerous."

We were equally impressed with the offerings at Bolton's, the other hot chicken standard-bearer in town. Outside, boxes of collards sat stacked, awaiting braising. Inside the tiny gray cinder-block structure, painted with sea-blue and red accents, you order your hot chicken (or fish) from a window with dimensions no larger than a sheet of printer paper. Monies are exchanged in advance, grape sodas purchased, and patience required as the chicken sizzles in the back. Finally, it emerges through the sliding window, white meat skewered on wooden sticks and nestled on a bed of crispy fries. Whereas Prince's spiciness has a slightly muskier, darker depth, Bolton's is all shrieking top notes, hitting the nasal passages with the sheer brute force of a sumo wrestler. With all that heat going on, it was surprising to tease out the nuances in flavor and style, but we left feeling we'd earned at least a beginner's certificate in hot chicken.

LEFT: Prince's Hot Chicken

OPPOSITE: Bolton's storefront and van; Josh Graham of Bolton's with a fresh skewer

ARNOLD'S COUNTRY KITCHEN FRIED CHICKEN,

Chicken Livers, Braised Turnip Greens, and Fried Green Tomatoes

SERVES 4

FOR THE BRINE

- 1 whole chicken, cut into 8 or 10 pieces
  Kosher salt and freshly ground black pepper

FOR THE WASH

- 5 large eggs
- ½ cup Louisiana-style hot sauce

FOR THE DREDGE

- 5 cups all-purpose flour, preferably White Lily brand
- 2 tablespoons kosher salt
- 1 tablespoon freshly ground black pepper
- 1 tablespoon freshly ground white pepper
- 1 teaspoon cayenne pepper
- 1 teaspoon granulated garlic
- 1 tablespoon poultry seasoning

  Canola oil, for frying

If there's one place you absolutely must *visit in Nashville, it's Arnold's Country Kitchen, a humble meat-and-three that brings the entire community to the table. It was founded by North Carolina native Jack Arnold in 1983; his eldest son, Khalil, now serves as chef and is constantly tweaking family recipes, like using horseradish and wasabi powder for heat and a touch of sugar to enhance the natural sweetness of his turnip greens. A line forms outside the long, narrow brick structure long before the doors open at 10:30 AM. From that moment until they close for the day at 2:30, the queue simply never lets up, inside snaking past shelves stacked with upside-down take-out containers waiting to be filled with the restaurant's famous sides. Everything on the rotating menu—from garlicky, fat-capped roast beef and stewed okra to a devilish, chili-laced chocolate pie—is to die for, but we came for the fried chicken—and it didn't disappoint. Available only on Mondays, it's the kind of crunchy, deeply satisfying bird you order in quantities and take home for leftovers. There's no reason food this simple should taste this good, but we're so grateful that it does.*

SEASON THE CHICKEN: Rinse the chicken in cold water and pat dry. Place the chicken in a Ziploc bag and season liberally with salt and pepper. Let chill while making the wash and dredge.

MAKE THE WASH AND DREDGE: In a large bowl, whisk together the eggs and hot sauce with 4 cups cold water. Refrigerate until cold, about 30 minutes. In a large bowl, whisk the flour with the salt, black pepper, white pepper, cayenne pepper, garlic, and poultry seasoning. (If making the fried chicken livers, reserve about 1½ cups of the dredge.) Fill a 12-inch cast-iron skillet with 2 inches oil and heat to 350°F.

FRY THE CHICKEN: Remove the wash from the refrigerator and dip the chicken in the wash, then press the chicken in the flour mixture and shake off the excess. Let the chicken rest on a plate, refrigerated, for 10 minutes, then re-press the chicken in the flour dredge. Line a platter with a cloth napkin or paper towels and set aside. Working in batches, place the chicken in the hot skillet and cook until the underside is golden brown, 7 to 8 minutes. Flip the chicken and cook until the other side is golden brown, an additional 7 to 8 minutes (some of the smaller pieces, like the legs and wings, will be done faster than the breasts or thighs). Place the chicken on the lined platter to drain. Season with additional salt, if desired, and serve hot or at room temperature.

FRIED CHICKEN LIVERS

SERVES 4-6

1 pound chicken livers
  Kosher salt and freshly ground black pepper
  Canola oil, for frying
1½ cups reserved flour dredge (see preceding recipe)

Rinse and pat dry the chicken livers and cut into 1- to 2-inch pieces. Season the chicken livers liberally with salt and pepper. Heat ¼ inch oil in a cast-iron skillet. Toss the chicken livers in the reserved flour dredge and panfry until extra crispy and deep brown, 2 to 3 minutes per side. Season with salt and pepper and serve hot.

A quick soak in a hot-sauce brine gives Arnold's fried chicken a kick. Though the Arnolds use White Lily brand all-purpose flour, any brand will do. We also adored their fried chicken livers (served at the restaurant with an onion gravy), which couldn't be simpler and use the same flour dredge as the chicken. If you're making the livers right after the chicken, use the leftover flour mix; if you make them on their own (see the recipe), a quarter of the flour dredge recipe is plenty.

ARNOLD'S

Monday

Roast Beef
ver & Onions
asa & Kraut
d Tilapia*
hicken*

Green Beans
Turnip Greens
Mashed Potatoes
Mac & Cheese
White Beans
Candied Yams
Boiled Cabbage
Small Salad

Tuesday

Roast Beef
Sugar Cured Ham
Meat Loaf
Chicken & Dumplings
Battered Grouper*

Green Beans
Turnip Greens
Mashed Potatoes
Mac & Cheese
Dressing
Black Eye
Bak

Wednesday

Roast Beef
Baked Chicken*
Fried Catfish*
Pork Chops*
Or
Brisket*

Thursday

Roast Beef
Chicken Livers & Rice
Country Fried Steak
Fried Shrimp*

Green
Tu

Roast Beef
Chicken &

Arnold's Country Kitchen's Fried Chicken

BRAISED TURNIP AND COLLARD GREENS

SERVES 4-6

Turnip greens can be hard to find outside the South, so look for them at Asian or Indian greengrocers, or ask your favorite vendor at the local farmers' market to sell you the greens that often get lopped off and discarded. If you can't find them, substitute with mustard greens. To make them vegetarian, omit the ham hock and bacon and use vegetarian bouillon instead of the ham base.

- 3 tablespoons margarine or unsalted butter
- 1 medium onion, chopped
- 2 pieces applewood-smoked bacon, chopped
- 1 medium (10-ounce) ham hock, chopped
- 1 medium turnip bulb (¾ pound), trimmed, peeled, and cut into ½-inch cubes
- 2 tablespoons prepared horseradish
- 2 tablespoons sugar
- 1 tablespoon kosher salt
- 2 teaspoons freshly ground black pepper
- 1 teaspoon crushed red pepper flakes
  Pinch of wasabi powder
- 1 tablespoon ham base
- 1 pound collard greens, stemmed and chopped
- 1 pound turnip or mustard greens, stemmed and chopped

Melt the margarine in a large, heavy pot over medium heat. Add the onion, bacon, and ham hock and cook until the onion is translucent, 5 to 6 minutes. Stir in the chopped turnip, horseradish, sugar, salt, black pepper, red pepper flakes, wasabi powder, ham base, and 6 cups water. Bring the liquid to a simmer, then add the greens in batches to let them wilt slightly. Cook, partially covered, over medium heat, stirring occasionally, until the greens and turnips are tender, 45 minutes to 1 hour (or longer, if desired), adding more water if necessary. Season with additional salt and pepper to taste.

FRIED GREEN TOMATOES

SERVES 4–6

2 cups all-purpose flour
¾ teaspoon kosher salt, plus more for seasoning
2 cups cornmeal
2 tablespoons dried basil
2 cups apple juice
5 large egg whites
   Dash of Tabasco sauce
5 green (unripe, not ripe heirloom) tomatoes
   (about 2 pounds), sliced into ¼-inch rounds
   Vegetable oil, for frying

In a shallow bowl, combine the flour and ½ teaspoon of the salt. Season the cornmeal liberally with salt and pepper. In a second bowl, combine the seasoned cornmeal, basil, and ¼ teaspoon of the salt. In a third bowl, whisk together the apple juice, egg whites, Tabasco sauce, and the remaining ¼ teaspoon salt.

Coat the tomato slices in the flour, shaking off the excess, then dip in the egg white mixture. Dip the eggy slices into the cornmeal-basil mixture.

Heat ¼ inch oil in a cast-iron skillet over medium-high heat. Fry the slices in batches until they are a deep golden brown, 2 to 3 minutes per side. Drain on paper towels, season with more salt to taste, and serve hot or at room temperature.

JOHN LASATER

HATTIE B'S HOT CHICKEN
SERVES 4

FOR THE DRY BRINE

- 1 whole chicken (3 pounds), washed, patted dry, and cut into quarters
- 1 tablespoon kosher salt
- 1½ teaspoons freshly ground black pepper

FOR THE DIP

- 1 cup whole milk
- 2 large eggs
- 1 tablespoon Louisiana-style hot sauce

FOR THE DREDGE

- 2 cups all-purpose flour
- 2 teaspoons sea salt

  Vegetable oil, for frying

FOR THE SPICY COATING

- ½ cup lard, melted and heated (or hot frying oil)
- 3 tablespoons cayenne pepper
- 1 tablespoon (packed) light brown sugar
- 1 teaspoon freshly ground black pepper
- ¾ teaspoon sea salt
- ½ teaspoon paprika
- ½ teaspoon garlic powder

Nashville is the nation's epicenter of hot chicken obsession, and closely held recipes for this fiery dish form one of our country's most secretive culinary subcultures. While respect for classic joints like Prince's and Bolton's only continues to crest, a crop of eager up-and-comers pay homage to the greats while adding their own heat-seeking twist. At Hattie B's, they offer their chicken in six—count 'em, six—descriptive levels of spiciness, from low-wattage Southern and Mild to dare-us-to-try-you Damn Hot and Shut the Cluck Up. The spicing in top-notch hot chicken is so aggressive that it assaults the taste buds at warp speed, but convincing a great practitioner to share a recipe was a process that moved at a decidedly slower pace. Thankfully Nick Bishop, owner of newcomer Hattie B's, and his chef, John Lasater, took pity on us—if not our palates—when they crafted this recipe with us in mind.

DRY BRINE THE CHICKEN: In a bowl, toss the chicken pieces with the salt and pepper, cover, and refrigerate overnight or up to 24 hours.

MAKE THE DIP AND DREDGE: In a bowl, whisk together the milk, eggs, and hot sauce. In a separate bowl, whisk together the flour and salt.

DREDGE THE CHICKEN: Dip the chicken in the flour mixture, then in the milk mixture, then in the flour mixture again, shaking off the excess after each step.

FRY THE CHICKEN: Fill a 6- to 8-quart pot halfway with oil and heat to 325°F. Set a wire rack on top of a rimmed baking sheet and set aside. Working in batches, lower the chicken into the fryer and fry until crisp, 15 to 17 minutes for breast quarters and 18 to 20 minutes for leg quarters. Remove the chicken and let drain on the rack.

MAKE THE SPICY COATING: Carefully ladle the lard or frying oil into a medium heatproof bowl and whisk in the cayenne pepper, brown sugar, black pepper, salt, paprika, and garlic powder. Baste the spice mixture over the hot fried chicken and serve immediately.

LEFT: Service with a smile from Jessica Ipina at Hattie B's

RIGHT: Chicken comes in six levels of heat, from "Southern" to "Shut the Cluck Up"

+ 1side + drink

D · MEDIUM
SHUT THE
CLUCK UP

FRIED CHICKEN *and* VELVETY MASHED POTATOES

SERVES 4

1 whole chicken, cut into 10 pieces
3 tablespoons kosher salt,
plus more to taste
3 cups all-purpose flour
2 tablespoons garlic powder
2 tablespoons onion powder
2 tablespoons paprika
2 teaspoons cayenne pepper
Freshly ground black pepper to taste
4 cups buttermilk
2 tablespoons hot sauce, preferably
Crystal or Tabasco
Peanut oil, for frying
¼ bunch fresh thyme
3 large sprigs fresh rosemary
¼ bunch fresh sage
½ head garlic (about 12 cloves),
smashed, husk still attached
Lemon wedges, for serving

I love nothing more than a simple, delicious, down-to-earth meal, and virtually all of Tyler Florence's food fits the bill . . . especially his fried chicken, which will always have a place at the top of my list. He may now live on the West Coast, but one bite of his chicken reminds you that his heart still resides in his hometown of Greenville, South Carolina. As part of a dinner he hosted at the 2012 Food Network New York City Wine & Food Festival, he served this dish, which brings together many of the best elements of the genre: brining, buttermilk batter, and double-dip in a heavily seasoned dredge. But what takes it over the edge is the oil he perfumes with fresh herbs and garlic—and the squeeze of fresh lemon—which infuses every bite with an extra layer of flavor.

BRINE THE CHICKEN: In a large (at least 5-quart) bowl or container, cover the chicken with 3 quarts cold water. Add 3 tablespoons salt, cover, and refrigerate at least 2 hours or overnight.

MAKE THE DREDGE: In a large shallow bowl, whisk together the flour, garlic powder, onion powder, paprika, cayenne pepper, and salt and black pepper to taste until well blended. In another large shallow bowl, whisk the buttermilk and hot sauce with a fork and season with salt and black pepper. Line a baking sheet with parchment and set aside.

DREDGE THE CHICKEN: Remove the chicken from the brine and pat it dry. Working a few pieces at a time, dredge the chicken pieces in the flour mixture, then dip them into the buttermilk, then dredge again in the seasoned flour. Set the pieces aside to rest on the parchment-lined sheet while you prepare the oil.

FRY THE HERBS: Pour about 3 inches oil into a large (at least 6-quart), deep pot. Add the thyme, rosemary, sage, and garlic to the cool oil and gradually heat over medium-high heat to between 360°F and 365°F on a deep-fry thermometer (the herbs and garlic will perfume the oil with their flavor as the oil heats).

FRY THE CHICKEN: Working in batches, add the chicken to the oil, 3 or 4 pieces at a time. Fry, turning the pieces once, until golden brown and cooked through, 12 to 13 minutes. Remove the chicken and herbs from the pot, shaking off as much oil as you can, and drain on a wire rack set over a rimmed baking sheet. Sprinkle all over with more salt and black pepper. Arrange the chicken on a platter and scatter the fried herbs and garlic over the top. Serve hot, with lemon wedges.

VELVETY MASHED POTATOES

SERVES 4

1 cup heavy cream
4 tablespoons unsalted butter
3 large Yukon Gold potatoes (2 ½ to 3 pounds), peeled
1 teaspoon kosher salt, plus more to taste
   Freshly ground black pepper to taste
¼ cup olive oil (optional)
   Chopped chives, for garnish

In a small saucepan, heat the cream and butter over medium heat until the butter melts; remove from the heat and set aside.

In a medium saucepan, cover the potatoes with cold water. Bring the pot to a boil, add the salt, reduce the heat, and simmer until the potatoes are very tender, 15 to 20 minutes. Drain, then pass the potatoes through a food mill or a ricer into a large mixing bowl. Gently stir in the warm cream and butter mixture until it is entirely absorbed by the potatoes and the mixture is smooth. Season with salt and pepper, then finish with the olive oil (if using). Garnish with chopped chives.

Tyler Florence's Fried Chicken and Velvety Mashed Potatoes

Charles Gabriel's Fried Chicken

HARD TO BELIEVE THAT SOME OF THE BEST, most authentic Southern fried chicken can be found smack in the middle of Harlem, but it's true. Day in and day out at his restaurant, Charles' Country Pan Fried Chicken, Charles Gabriel makes the Southern food of his childhood for a crowd of neighborhood regulars and an ever-growing legion of fans from the far reaches of Manhattan and beyond.

The son of sharecroppers from Huntersville, North Carolina, Gabriel grew up working the cotton fields with his twelve siblings, then coming home every night to a dinner made by his mother, Nora Bell. For Nora Bell's fried chicken, the kids would kill yardbirds raised on the property; vegetables were grown in the backyard, and yams were nestled in the straw-lined root cellar in the winter. Nora Bell reserved making fried chicken for weekends and special occasions when there was a little more time for both cooking and eating, frying it in batches and setting it atop the icebox until dinner. "We always snuck a fresh piece or two," remembered Gabriel, "no matter how many times she slapped our hands." He made his way to New York at age 17, at first helping out at his older brother's restaurant before working his way up the ladder at Copeland's, a Southern cooking institution on 145th Street. Eventually he struck out on his own, frying out of his home kitchen and selling his chicken, first off a folding table on a street corner, then out of a catering truck that drew crowds and critical acclaim. He eventually established his current location, which has operated pretty much without interruption since 1985. When cooking, Charles takes his time; this is "slow food" without the posturing.

OPPOSITE: Facing the kitchen at Charles' Country Pan Fried Chicken in Harlem

Charles at work battering his birds and frying them up in his cast-iron skillet. Long-handled, coal-black, and capable of handling twenty-five pieces of chicken at a time, the imposing vessel easily covers all four of the stovetop burners. No deep fryer here; Charles believes a pool of oil leaches flavor from the chicken, whereas a skillet allows chicken to bathe in its own juices. "Less oil, less grease," he said. "Most importantly, you can't walk away from the chicken. It requires your attention."

CHARLES GABRIEL

COUNTRY PAN FRIED CHICKEN
and Candied Yams

SERVES 4

1 whole chicken, cut into 8 pieces
1 tablespoon kosher salt
½ teaspoon freshly ground
  black pepper
1 teaspoon garlic powder
  Soybean or canola oil, for frying
2 cups whole milk
3 large eggs
2 cups all-purpose flour

"I've been making fried chicken since I was nine or ten," said Charles Gabriel, owner of Charles' Country Pan Fried Chicken, as he kept watch over the largest cast-iron skillet we'd ever seen. When frying his birds, Gabriel morphs into a human rotisserie, constantly rotating the pieces with tongs and demonstrating an innate understanding of the microclimates that exist within the high sides of the skillet.

With his starched chef's jacket and chef's toque—not to mention his considerable girth and height—this Charles is most certainly in charge, spending several hours a day personally buying produce for the made-in-house sides including corn bread, collards, and candied yams. But in the end the star is still the chicken, which establishes the perfect balance between levity and crunch.

SEASON THE CHICKEN: In a bowl or Ziploc bag, season the chicken with the salt, pepper, and garlic powder. Cover or seal and refrigerate overnight or up to 24 hours. Pour 1 inch oil into a 12-inch cast-iron skillet and heat until a pinch of flour sizzles upon contact (355–360°F). Set a rack over a rimmed baking sheet and set aside. In a bowl, whisk together the milk and eggs. Place the flour in a separate bowl. Dip the chicken in the egg wash, drain off the excess, then dredge in the flour, shaking off the excess.

FRY THE CHICKEN: Place the chicken, skin side down, in the skillet and fry in batches for 3 minutes without moving. Continue to fry, turning the chicken every 1 to 2 minutes to ensure even browning and cooking, until the chicken is cooked through, 13 to 15 minutes. Drain on the rack and serve hot, warm, or at room temperature.

CANDIED YAMS

SERVES 6

4 pounds yams, preferably the larger,
  light orange-skinned variety (3 or 4 yams), scrubbed
2 cups sugar
½ orange
2 cinnamon sticks
½ teaspoon kosher salt
1 cup (2 sticks) unsalted butter, cubed, plus more for greasing

In a large, heavy pot, cover the yams with water. Bring to a boil, reduce the heat, and simmer until tender but not falling apart, 25 to 30 minutes. Remove from the heat, cool the yams, remove the skins, and dice into ½-inch pieces. In a saucepan, combine 4 cups water with the sugar, orange, cinnamon sticks, and salt. Bring the water to a boil, then reduce the heat to medium and simmer until a thick, but still pourable, syrup forms, 35 to 37 minutes. Remove the orange and cinnamon sticks.

Preheat the oven to 350°F. Generously butter the bottom of an 9 × 13-inch glass baking dish. Place the dish on a rimmed baking sheet. Arrange the diced yams in the dish. Carefully pour the syrup on top of the yams, then top with the cubes of butter. Bake until the syrup has been absorbed and the top edges are slightly browned, 50 minutes to 1 hour.

FRIED CHICKEN *and* HASH BROWN CASSEROLE

SERVES 4

1 whole chicken, cut into 8 pieces
  Kosher salt, for brining
1 cup self-rising flour
1 tablespoon seasoned salt
½ teaspoon freshly ground
  black pepper
1¼ teaspoons garlic powder
  Canola oil, peanut oil, or lard,
  for frying

In 1951, the Loveless Café, about a 30-minute drive outside downtown Nashville, was founded as a motel and restaurant designed to feed travelers rolling by on Highway 100, a road that lazily winds down to Natchez, Mississippi. Many a famed musician's tour bus has pulled over for a dose of Southern comfort (and we suspect, Southern Comfort); legend has it the Loveless was where the late, great George Jones came to sober up after a particularly long bender. Though it's gone through several owners, the Loveless's delicious fried chicken has been a constant. Flash-brined, dusted in self-rising flour, and fried in your choice of fats to a state of heavenly crispness, it's everything fried chicken should be. The hash brown casserole is sinfully rich and unabashedly made from pantry staples; one of its main ingredients—a can of condensed cream soup—has been half-jokingly referred to as the "duct tape of the Southern kitchen." Served up with a few fried eggs and a piece of crisp chicken, it's Southern hangover food done right.

PREPARE THE CHICKEN: Rinse the chicken under cold water, then submerge in cold, heavily salted water for at least 30 minutes. Drain and thoroughly pat dry with paper towels. In a bowl, whisk together the flour, seasoned salt, pepper, and garlic powder.

DREDGE AND FRY THE CHICKEN: In a large (at least 12-inch) skillet with a tight-fitting lid, heat 1 inch oil to 375°F. Dredge the chicken in the seasoned flour, coating well on all surfaces. Shake off the excess breading and place the chicken in the hot oil, making sure the pieces are not touching each other, and cook until the underside begins to brown, about 5 minutes. Flip the chicken, reduce the heat to 300°F, then cover and cook until deeply browned, 20 minutes. Remove the lid, return the heat to 300°F, then flip the chicken and cook until crisp, an additional 5 to 7 minutes. Drain on paper towels before eating.

HASH BROWN CASSEROLE

SERVES 8–10

1   30-ounce (or 2 16-ounce) bags shredded refrigerated
    hash brown potatoes, defrosted if frozen
1   large yellow onion, finely chopped
1   8-ounce bag shredded Cheddar cheese (about 2 cups)
1   10¾-ounce can cream of chicken soup
2   cups sour cream
2   teaspoons kosher salt
½   teaspoon freshly ground black pepper

For a bit of extra flavor, brown the shredded potatoes in some hot vegetable oil for 4 to 5 minutes before combining with the other ingredients.

Preheat the oven to 400°F. Lightly butter a 9 × 13-inch casserole dish and set aside.

In a large bowl, combine all ingredients until well mixed. Transfer to the prepared dish and bake, covered with tin foil, until the edges begin to brown, about 30 minutes. Remove the tin foil and continue to bake until completely golden brown, an additional 30 to 40 minutes.

Origin[ally] on Highw[ay] motel rooms for we[ary]

As the outskirts of Nashville ex[pand] (including the secret biscuit rec[ipe] the Loveless Cafe experience

With the introduction of the could no longer keep up w[ith] for restorations. Today th[e]

The Lovele[ss]

```
K K Y E C A
U E U S A M
S F L R R F
N A W E O E
E M B L L A
E I I B F H
R L S B A T
G Y C O Y D
P S U C A E
I T I R S C A
N Y T E K N R
R L S E A Y Y V
U E N N O S T R
T L A H T O L C E
D B C B Y E N I H S
```

How many of these

The Loveless Café's Fried Chicken and Hash Brown Casserole

Scenes from inside and outside the Loveless Café

"NAKED" FRIED CHICKEN
and Old-Fashioned Coleslaw

SERVES 8

FOR THE BRINE

1 cup kosher salt
2 whole chickens (ideally 2½ pounds each), each cut into 10 pieces

FOR THE CHICKEN

3 cups lard
3 cups peanut oil
½ cup (1 stick) unsalted butter
4 ounces country ham slices or scraps
3 ounces smoked bacon (4 to 6 slices, depending on thickness)
8 cups all-purpose flour
1 cup cornstarch
1 tablespoon kosher salt
2 tablespoons freshly ground black pepper

Hopkins believes fried chicken is best served at room temperature or cold, giving the chicken time to rest allows it to reabsorb its juices.

"This is the food of memory, history, and family," Linton Hopkins told us as we sat down to platters of fried chicken at one of his Atlanta restaurants, Holeman & Finch. Hopkins was raised on Southern food, spending lazy weekends on the porch eating his grandfather's fried chicken. Originally a pre-med major at Emory, Hopkins realized that his true calling was to reinterpret his family's food for a new generation.
"I like to call this naked chicken," said Hopkins of his birds. He peeled the crispy skin and juicy meat from a moist, juicy breast, as if he were separating the layers of an onion. A proponent of using "fat, little happy birds" for frying, Hopkins eschews buttermilk dredges and heavy coating. "When the fatty skin touches the direct heat of frying with no barriers, it creates caramelization," he told us. "The skin fries up like cracklings."

Our chicken came with a surprise: chasers of ice-cold Cruze Dairy buttermilk, a brand typically available only in the South. "As a kid we used to drink buttermilk with fried chicken," said Hopkins, and once we downed the light, tangy liquid we understood why. The buttermilk cut through the richness of the chicken, cleansing our palates for the next stop on our fried chicken road trip. Who knew? Dr. Hopkins, of course.

BRINE THE CHICKEN: In a large bowl or resealable container, whisk the salt with 3 quarts water until dissolved. Add the chicken, cover, and refrigerate for 24 hours. Remove the chicken from the brine and pat dry.

COOK THE HAM AND BACON: Set a wire rack over a rimmed baking sheet and set aside. Combine the lard and peanut oil in a large (at least 6-quart) cast-iron Dutch oven or other heavy pot and gently heat to 200°F. Add the butter, ham, and bacon and cook for 15 minutes to flavor the oil, then remove and discard the ham and bacon. Heat the fat until it reaches 340°F to 350°F.

(continued)

DREDGE THE CHICKEN: In a large bowl, whisk together the flour, cornstarch, salt, and pepper. Toss the chicken in the flour mixture, shaking off the excess.

FRY THE CHICKEN: Working in batches, gently lay the chicken pieces in the oil and fry till golden brown and cooked through, turning to promote uniform browning, 15 to 17 minutes for breasts, 13 to 14 minutes for thighs, and 11 to 12 minutes for wings and drumsticks. Drain on the rack and let the chicken rest for at least 30 minutes before serving.

HOLEMAN AND FINCH
PUBLIC HOUSE

OPPOSITE: Linton Hopkins

ABOVE: Hopkins's "naked" fried chicken

LEFT: Peeling away the layers to reveal moist, tender chicken

OLD-FASHIONED COLESLAW

SERVES 8

Hopkins salts and drains his cabbage, which allows it to absorb the sweet and tart dressing. We find that this coleslaw only gets better with age, so don't worry if there are leftovers.

1	head (about 2½ pounds) green cabbage, very thinly shredded
2	teaspoons kosher salt, plus more for seasoning
2	medium carrots, grated
1	medium red onion, thinly sliced
2	scallions (white and green parts), chopped
1½	cups homemade (or store-bought) mayonnaise
¼	cup Dijon mustard
6	tablespoons apple cider vinegar
	Juice of 1 large lemon
6	tablespoons sugar
½	teaspoon celery seed
½	teaspoon cayenne pepper
	Freshly ground black pepper to taste

In a large bowl, toss the cabbage with the salt. Cover with cold water, cover the bowl, and refrigerate for 4 hours.

Drain the cabbage well, using a towel to squeeze out extra water. In a large bowl combine the cabbage, carrots, red onion, and scallions. In another bowl, whisk together the mayonnaise, mustard, vinegar, lemon juice, sugar, celery seed, and cayenne pepper. Add the dressing to the vegetables and toss to coat. Season with additional salt and pepper to taste.

JACQUES-IMO'S FRIED CHICKEN
and Smothered Cabbage

SERVES 4

1 whole chicken, cut into 8 pieces
  Salt and freshly ground white pepper
  to taste
  Canola or safflower oil, for frying
4 large eggs
½ cup evaporated milk
1½ teaspoons Worcestershire sauce
2 cups all-purpose flour
½ cup chopped fresh flat-leaf parsley
¼ cup minced fresh garlic
  Ruffled dill pickle slices

With décor seemingly lifted from a psychedelic dreamscape—not to mention N'awlins-on-'roids menu items like alligator cheesecake—it would be easy to dismiss Jacques-Imo's, in New Orleans's Uptown neighborhood, as an easily skippable tourist magnet. What a mistake that would be. Behind the cheerfully organized chaos, chef/owner Jacques Leonardi has been serving plates of crispy bird made with a recipe handed down by NOLA's now-deceased patron chef-saint of fried chicken, Austin Leslie. Leslie plied his trade for decades, owning several restaurants in town and even becoming the inspiration for a short-lived 1987 TV series, Frank's Place. But when his own restaurants fell upon hard times, he showed up at Leonardi's door ready to work—which he did until his death in 2004. Evaporated milk and white pepper—Leslie's signature ingredients—add lightness and subtle spice; his memory adds something altogether intangible. At the restaurant, Leonardi's smothered cabbage is a standout; he uses alligator sausage and a house-made spice blend, but andouille and any good-quality Cajun seasoning mix will do.

SEASON THE CHICKEN: Season the chicken liberally with salt and white pepper, place in a Ziploc bag, and refrigerate overnight.

DREDGE THE CHICKEN: Prepare a deep-fryer or fill a large (at least 8-quart) pot halfway with oil and heat to 350°F. In a large bowl, whisk together the eggs, evaporated milk, Worcestershire sauce, and salt to taste. In a separate bowl, season the flour with salt to taste. Dip the chicken in the egg wash, then coat in the seasoned flour, shaking off the excess. Working in batches, fry the chicken until golden and crisp, 11 to 12 minutes for the wings and drumsticks, 15 to 16 minutes for thighs, and 19 to 20 minutes for the breasts. Drain on paper towels.

TO SERVE: Garnish with the chopped parsley, minced garlic, and pickles. Serve with the smothered cabbage on the side.

SMOTHERED CABBAGE

MAKES ABOUT 8 CUPS

FOR THE CAJUN SEASONING (MAKES 1¼ CUPS)

- ¼ cup kosher salt
- 6 tablespoons paprika
- 2 tablespoons freshly ground black pepper
- 2 tablespoons freshly ground white pepper
- 2 tablespoons garlic powder
- 2 tablespoons onion powder
- 1 tablespoon dried thyme
- 1 tablespoon cayenne pepper

FOR THE CABBAGE

- 4 tablespoons margarine or unsalted butter
- 1 large onion, chopped
- 2 links alligator or andouille sausage, sliced into ⅛-inch rounds
- 4 cups chicken stock
- 1 small green cabbage (about 2½ pounds), sliced into ½-inch-thick shreds
- ½ red cabbage (about 1¼ pounds), sliced into ½-inch-thick shreds

MAKE THE CAJUN SEASONING: In a medium bowl, whisk together all ingredients. Transfer to an airtight container. (The leftover Cajun seasoning will keep for 6 months.)

MAKE THE CABBAGE: Heat the margarine in a large pot over medium-high heat. Add the onion and sausage and cook, stirring, until the onion is golden brown, 9 to 10 minutes. Reduce the temperature, add 1½ tablespoons Cajun seasoning, and cook, stirring occasionally, until the onion and sausage are very soft and browned, an additional 10 to 12 minutes. Add 1 cup of the stock and cook until nearly evaporated, 4 to 5 minutes.

Add the green and red cabbage and the remaining 3 cups stock. Raise the heat to medium-high and cook, stirring, until the cabbage fades in color but still retains a slight crunch, 18 to 20 minutes.

ABOVE: Jacques Leonardi

RIGHT: The dining room at Jacques-Imo's

McHardy's, Willie Mae's, and Dooky Chase's

NEW ORLEANS AND FRIED CHICKEN GO TOGETHER like red beans and rice, a fact confirmed after a couple of days in the Crescent City. Two establishments, Dooky Chase's and Willie Mae's Scotch House, loom large in fried chicken mythology here, but we found a city filled with memorable versions of fried chicken, many of them humble stand-alone institutions helping to tell the city's story.

When we stopped in unannounced at McHardy's Chicken & Fixin', owner Alvi Anderson-Mogilles was pleased as punch to see us. "I'm the Colonel here," said Alvi, 61, a former school administrator who persuaded her husband, Kermit, to leave his successful banking career and open McHardy's in 2004. Defying Katrina's devastation, they reopened at the end of 2006, determined to help the city get back on its feet, one five-order box at a time. "Feeding people took on more meaning," she told us. Alvi insists on rinsing and chilling her chicken ("It's got to be cold!"), then coating it in a secret blend of spiced flour, a recipe handed down from her late mother (we detected strong hints of lemon pepper and ground celery seed). McHardy's also participates in a prison work-release program, helping inmates readjust to life on the outside after incarceration. "Frying chicken is a journey," Alvi told us as she sent us on our way with a to-go box. "I'm just along for the ride."

Arriving at Willie Mae's Scotch House, we were looking forward as much to a true taste of New Orleans history as we were to the fried chicken. Willie Mae Seaton first opened a restaurant in 1956 in the French Quarter,

---

OPPOSITE and **FOLLOWING PAGE:** Scenes from McHardy's Chicken & Fixin'

TOP: Owner Alvi Anderson-Mogilles and her son Rahman

moving a year later to its current location in the Seventh Ward. Admiration for her classic Creole dishes grew over time, as did her reputation as an equal-opportunity provider: freedom riders, politicians, musicians, and regular folk were all welcome. But it was her fried chicken people crowed for, stopping in during Jazz Fest, before a Saints game, or after church to savor it. Then came Katrina, and just like that fifty years of hard work were seemingly in peril. Your average 88-year-old might have taken it as a sign, but Willie Mae was determined to reopen. With the help of chefs like John Besh and John Currence and organizations including the James Beard Foundation and the Southern Foodways Alliance, Willie Mae's rebuilt, expanded, and reopened within eighteen months of the storm.

On the day of our visit, a velvet rope stood at the ready for crowd control, a necessity for the lunchtime rush. Though it was only seven years old, the main dining room, decorated with posters of African

American legends ranging from Jelly Roll Morton to Barack Obama, had a lived-in feel. Willie Mae, now 98 years old, has handed over the reins to her very capable great-granddaughter, Kerry Seaton Blackmon. Kerry managed the staff with a smiling but commanding presence, and shooed us away when we asked after Willie Mae's carefully guarded recipe. Instead, she sent a feast to our table; the corn bread and red beans merely supporting players to that chicken, a lacy, multilayered, physics-defying crust enrobing juicy, well-seasoned meat.

And then, finally, we arrived at Dooky Chase's, just as lunch was ending. Waiters cleared tables topped with white tablecloths under walls hung with African American art. Out came Mrs. Leah Chase, more radiant at 91 than we could hope to be at any age, her gait slow but her voice strong and clear. Young Leah fell into the restaurant business when she married Edgar "Dooky" Chase in 1946. He was an experimental jazz musician whose parents

OPPOSITE: Kerry Seaton Blackmon at Willie Mae's Scotch House

LEFT and **ABOVE:** Scenes from inside and outside Willie Mae's

Willie Mae's Fried Chicken and Fixings

owned the restaurant. She eventually remade the place to her liking, introducing Creole dishes that to this day are New Orleans classics: gumbo, stuffed chicken, redfish Orleans. Serving good food wasn't enough for Leah Chase, and she decorated Dooky's with fine dining touches: knife rests, a parlor with marble tables, and elegant chafing dishes. "What do you do when company is coming?" she asked. "You bring out the best you have." In the 1960s, Dooky Chase's became a gathering place for civil rights activists, freedom riders, even James Baldwin; they all debated the issues and made their plans over plates of gumbo and fried chicken. Still, Mrs. Chase had her standards. If they came to the door dirty, she sent them to take showers.

Through the rise of fast food and inelegant service, Dooky Chase's has persisted. "People took a chance on me and helped me along," she said. "I try to do the same." Like so many others, Katrina nearly wiped out Dooky Chase's. But the community rallied to raise money to rebuild, and they reopened in 2007. "I'm still not where I want to be," she said, lamenting the lack of properly trained staff available for hire. "But as long as I can, I will keep on going," she concluded. "Because this place is about so much more than the food."

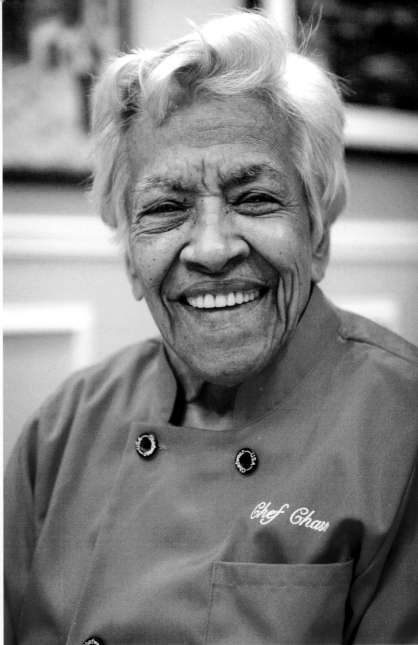

Leah Chase and her famously fancy bird at Dooky Chase's

SUNDAY NIGHT FRIED CHICKEN
and Lake Charles Dirty Rice

SERVES 4–6

FOR THE CHICKEN

- 1 whole chicken, cut into 10 pieces, with wing-on breast halves
- 2 teaspoons kosher salt
- 1 teaspoon freshly ground black pepper
- ½ teaspoon cayenne pepper
- ¼ teaspoon freshly ground white pepper
- ½ teaspoon garlic powder
- 5 dashes Louisiana hot sauce
- 1 cup buttermilk
- 3 cups lard, vegetable shortening, bacon fat, or a combination of the three, for frying
- 3 cups all-purpose flour

FOR THE RICE

- 2 tablespoons canola oil
- 4 ounces ground pork
- 4 ounces raw chicken liver, puréed (½ cup)
- 1½ teaspoons kosher salt
- ½ teaspoon freshly ground black pepper
- ½ teaspoon chili powder
- 1½ cups chicken stock
- 1 small onion, finely chopped (1 cup)
- 2 celery stalks, finely chopped (½ cup)
- 1 or 2 jalapeño peppers, seeds and ribs included, finely chopped
- 2 garlic cloves, minced
- 1 tablespoon dried oregano
- 3 cups cooked white rice
- 4 scallions (white and green parts), chopped (1 cup), plus more for garnish
- 2 tablespoons chopped parsley, plus more for garnish

ON THE PASS-THROUGH BETWEEN the open kitchen and the dining room at Donald Link's New Orleans restaurant, Cochon, there sits an enviable collection of cast-iron vessels, used nightly to prepare Link's modern-traditional take on Cajun cooking. Link's understandably popular fried chicken, a too-infrequent special on Cochon's menu, is made just like his granny used to make it in Lake Charles: seasoned, skillet-fried, dark, and so crunchy that each bite practically echoes through the large, wood-accented dining room. The recipe calls for a mix of fats, but don't fret if you end up using just one. And once it's out of the skillet, slow down: Link believes that waiting up to 20 minutes allows the bird's natural chicken juices to settle. Take the extra time to make that dirty rice: the introduction of puréed liver lends an earthy depth to the dish (and fools the liver-averse every time).

For Link's recipe, cutting the chicken into ten pieces instead of the more typical eight (two wings, two breasts, two drumsticks, two thighs) results in smaller, easy-to-hold pieces with more crispy goodness. Cut the chicken into eight pieces (or buy a presectioned chicken), leaving the breast side of the wing attached. Cut the breast in half, making ten pieces, which gives you two wings, two thighs, two legs, and four pieces of breast—two with the drumstick side of the wing attached.

SEASON THE CHICKEN: In a large bowl, toss the chicken with the salt, black pepper, cayenne pepper, white pepper, garlic powder, and hot sauce until evenly coated. Cover with plastic wrap and refrigerate for at least 1 hour or up to 1 day (the longer the better, to allow the seasonings to permeate the meat).

DREDGE THE CHICKEN: Transfer the chicken to a clean mixing bowl and pour the buttermilk over the chicken. Heat the frying fat of your choice in a large (12-inch) cast-iron skillet to 350°F, or until a pinch of flour sizzles when dropped into the fat. As the oil heats, remove the chicken from the buttermilk, allowing excess liquid to drip off, and transfer to a clean bowl. Add the flour and toss to coat.

FRY THE CHICKEN: When the oil is ready, working in batches and starting with the larger cuts, add the chicken pieces to the skillet, shaking off any excess flour before placing in the oil. (Make sure not to overcrowd the pan.) Fry the chicken pieces, turning with tongs occasionally and making sure the oil maintains a mellow sizzle, 8 minutes per side. Transfer the chicken to a plate lined with paper towels to soak up the excess oil. Let the chicken sit for 20 minutes while you make the rice.

MAKE THE RICE: In a large, heavy skillet, heat the oil over high heat. Add the pork and liver and cook, stirring, until browned, 3 to 4 minutes. Stir in the salt, pepper, and chili powder to combine. Add ¼ cup of the chicken stock and cook until evaporated, allowing the meat mixture to get browned and crusty once again and stick to the pan, an additional 5 to 6 minutes. (Resist the impulse to stir constantly: you want the meat to stick to the pan and get nice and crusty.)

Add the onion, celery, jalapeño, garlic, and oregano and cook, stirring, until the vegetables are nicely browned and crusty and begin to stick to the pan, about 4 minutes. Add the remaining 1¼ cups stock and the rice, scallions, and parsley and stir until the liquid is absorbed and the rice is heated through, 3 to 4 minutes.

Season with salt and pepper to taste and garnish with additional scallions and parsley, if desired. Serve the chicken with the dirty rice on the side.

Donald Link's Sunday Night Fried Chicken and Lake Charles Dirty Rice

Kermit's Treme Speakeasy Restaurant

ONLY IN NEW ORLEANS would you find an award-winning jazz musician with his own club, complete with a secret-weapon cook who fries up some of the best-tasting chicken in town. Then again, only in New Orleans would you find Kermit Ruffins. "Kermit's getting worked on," said the man calling himself Dirty Rice who stood in front of Kermit's Treme Speakeasy Restaurant in New Orleans's Seventh Ward, before breaking into a cavernous smile punctuated by several gold-capped teeth. Nearby, his associates sold T-shirts from a folding table as a barbecue emitted a slow, steady trail of smoke. While Kermit's restaurant closed in early 2014, the memories of our visit there are indelible, a true only-in-N'Awlins experience.

We walked in to find Ruffins—trumpeter extraordinaire, regular on the late, great television series *Treme*, and lifelong resident of New Orleans—inverted into one of those padded ten-minute-massage chairs, stripped down to a ribbed white tank and jeans, arms dangling by his sides. "He'll be with you in a few minutes," said a waitress. "Want to talk to Boom Boom?"

Chef Ray "Boom Boom" (like Madonna or Bono, no last name necessary) and Kermit first met as musicians at different local high schools. Ray cooked for years at local restaurants including Bart's Lighthouse (now Landry's) and Mike Anderson's before running his own joint-cum-club, Ray's Boom-Boom Room, for twenty years. "I used to work for Austin Leslie," he said, referring to New Orleans's deceased pied piper of fried chicken (see the Jacques-Imo's recipe on page 73). "Eventually Austin worked for me." Hurricane Katrina led to the demise of many good restaurants in New Orleans, especially smaller, neighborhood ones, including, eventually, the

OPPOSITE: (left) Kermit and Ray Boom Boom; (right) Dirty Rice

CLOCKWISE FROM TOP: Kermit Ruffins on stage; Kermit's trumpet on the stovetop; Boom Boom's simple, secret ingredient

OPPOSITE: Kermit and Boom Boom's "hard-fried" chicken

Boom-Boom Room. But during the restaurant's long tenure Ray perfected his recipe for "hard fried" chicken, where nothing stands between the chicken and salty dredge. "My mom and grandma weren't wasting eggs or even buttermilk on fried chicken," he said. "That was breakfast food." He took us back into the spotless kitchen and made quick work of tossing baking powder, salt, pepper, and Morton's Season All into a bowl. "Chicken's got to be rinsed, dried, and chilled," he said as he dredged a cold bird and threw it straight into the deep-fryer.

When it was done, we took our paper plates back out into the restaurant where Kermit, dressed in a mint-green chef's coat and matching porkpie cap, was finally ready for us. "I'm forty-eight years old and I finally have a day job," he laughed, beer in hand (one thing you quickly learn about Kermit is that he always has a beer in hand). Born and raised in the Lower Ninth, Kermit moved to the Treme when he founded the Rebirth Brass Band in 1983, then the Barbecue All Stars in 1992. His second band's name is an indication of just how inexorably bonded music and good food are in this town. Kermit grew up in a food-loving home where his mother, Esther May, raised goats for slaughter and had a vegetable garden. Though he caught the music bug young, Kermit never lost his interest in good eating. To this day, he makes his own barbecue before every show—hence that green chef's coat—giving it away for free to patrons who could just as easily pay for Boom Boom's fried chicken. "Life is one long picnic," he told us just before changing clothes and taking the stage for the night's first set. "If you look at it that way, everything's just a little bit easier."

HARD-FRIED CHICKEN

SERVES 4

3 ½ cups all-purpose flour
 ½ cup all-purpose seasoning, such as
     Morton's Season All
  2 tablespoons baking powder
  1 tablespoon freshly ground black
     pepper
     Vegetable oil, for frying
  1 whole chicken, washed, patted dry,
     cut into 8 pieces, and well chilled
     Sea salt

Perhaps because the chicken is deeply chilled before frying, Boom Boom cooks his chicken a little longer than most; it emerges with the signature "hard-fried" brittle crust, notable for aggressively salty seasoning.

MAKE THE DREDGE: In a large bowl, combine the flour, seasoning, baking powder, and pepper.

FRY THE CHICKEN: Prepare a deep-fryer or fill a large (at least 6-quart) pot halfway with oil and heat to 355°F to 360°F. Dredge the chicken in the flour mixture, shake off the excess, and fry until the chicken is dark brown and the crust is brittle, 16 to 18 minutes. Drain on paper towels and season with salt to taste.

ELIZABETH KARMEL

HILL COUNTRY BUTTERMILK FRIED CHICKEN,
Cheesy Garlic Grits, and Candied Country Ham

SERVES 4

FOR THE BUTTERMILK BRINE

1 cup kosher salt

1 cup (packed) dark brown sugar

3 large sprigs fresh rosemary, or 2 tablespoons dried

1 generous teaspoon cracked black peppercorns

2 cups ice cubes

4 cups cold buttermilk

1 teaspoon cayenne pepper

1 whole chicken, washed, patted dry, cut into 8 pieces, and trimmed of excess fat

FOR THE SEASONED FLOUR

2½ cups White Lily flour (or all-purpose flour)

1 tablespoon kosher salt

2 teaspoons coarsely ground black pepper

2 teaspoons garlic powder

2 teaspoons onion powder

2 teaspoons smoked Spanish paprika

Meet Elizabeth Karmel, the trailblazing woman who single-handedly conquered two male-dominated arenas of the food world through sheer determination and talent. She followed up her hugely successful barbecue empire, anchored at New York's incomparable Hill Country, with Hill Country Chicken, which is dedicated to immaculately fried and expertly seasoned birds. Elizabeth's chicken combines elements of her mother's classic recipe, but the seasoning is all her own; make sure to sprinkle it on while the bird is still hot so it adheres well and really permeates the chicken. The cheesy, long-cooked grits are worth the constant stirring, and the candied ham is what Elizabeth calls "the bow on a package," balancing the savory components in the grits and chicken to create the optimal salty-sweet experience.

MAKE THE BRINE: In a large saucepan, bring the salt, sugar, rosemary, peppercorns, and 3 cups hot water to a boil, stirring to dissolve the sugar and salt. Remove from the heat and cool for 15 minutes. Add the ice cubes, buttermilk, and cayenne pepper; whisk to incorporate, and let rest until the brine is cool to the touch. Transfer the brine to a heavy-duty brining bag or a nonreactive food-safe container with a lid. Submerge the chicken in the brine; cover and refrigerate for 2 hours—no more, or the chicken will be too salty.

MAKE THE SEASONED FLOUR: In a large bowl, whisk together the flour, salt, pepper, garlic powder, onion powder, and paprika.

MAKE THE CHICKEN SHAKE SEASONING: In a medium bowl, whisk all the ingredients together.

FRY THE CHICKEN: Fill a large (12-inch) cast-iron skillet with a tight-fitting lid with about 1½ inches oil and heat to 325°F. Arrange 2 racks over 2 rimmed baking sheets and set aside. Remove the chicken from the brine; shake off the excess liquid

FOR THE SWEET AND SPICY CHICKEN SHAKE SEASONING

- ⅓ cup (packed) dark brown sugar
- 2 tablespoons kosher salt
- 2 tablespoons smoked Spanish paprika
- 1 tablespoon paprika
- 1 tablespoon freshly ground black pepper
- 1 tablespoon freshly ground white pepper
- 2 teaspoons garlic powder
- 2 teaspoons onion powder
- 1 teaspoon celery salt
- ½ teaspoon cayenne pepper

Peanut oil, for frying

and coat evenly in the flour mixture. Let sit for 5 minutes on a rack, coat again with the flour mixture, and immediately place the chicken, bone side down, in the skillet. Cover and fry until the bottom is golden brown and the top is beginning to cook, about 10 minutes. Remove the lid, flip the chicken, and then cover the skillet and let cook until the chicken is almost done, an additional 5 minutes. Remove the lid and fry uncovered until the skin is crisp, an additional 3 to 4 minutes. (It will take a total of 15 to 20 minutes to cook, depending on the size of the chicken pieces. If you turn only once, larger pieces may take longer.)

TO SERVE: Drain the chicken on the second rack, sprinkle with the Chicken Shake seasoning to taste, and keep warm in the oven until ready to serve. Serve the chicken with the grits; sprinkle the candied ham on top or serve it on the side.

Extra Chicken Shake seasoning can be stored in an airtight container for up to 6 months.

If you don't have a candy thermometer, you can gauge the oil's readiness by dropping a cube of bread in the oil. If it floats and immediately starts to bubble and brown on the edges, then the oil is at the right temperature.

Elizabeth Karmel's Hill Country Buttermilk Chicken
with Cheesy Garlic Grits and Candied Country Ham

CHEESY GARLIC GRITS

SERVES 4–6

1	cup heavy whipping cream
1½	cups coarse-ground grits, preferably white, such as Anson Mills or Bob's Red Mill
1	cup (4 ounces) freshly grated white Cheddar cheese
1½	cups freshly grated Parmigiano-Reggiano cheese
2	tablespoons unsalted butter
1	teaspoon kosher salt, or more to taste
½	teaspoon garlic powder
¼	teaspoon freshly ground black pepper
	Tabasco sauce to taste

In a 4-quart saucepan, bring 2¾ cups water and the cream to a gentle boil. Gradually add the grits and simmer, stirring often and alternating between cooking with the lid on for 15 minutes, then cooking uncovered for 15 minutes, until the grits are soft but still al dente and have a little resistance but are not mushy, about 1 hour. (Add water by the tablespoonful if the grits are too stiff.) Stir in the cheeses, butter, salt, garlic powder, pepper, and Tabasco sauce. Adjust seasonings to taste.

CANDIED COUNTRY HAM

MAKES 2 CUPS

Phillips Brothers biscuit-cut country ham can be purchased online from Julia's Pantry. If you can't find it or order it, you can substitute thick slices of good-quality Virginia ham from your local deli counter.

- ⅔ cup granulated sugar
- ⅓ cup (packed) dark brown sugar
- 1 teaspoon kosher salt
- ½ teaspoon ground cinnamon
  Generous pinch of cayenne pepper
- 1 pound center-cut slices biscuit-cut country ham, such as Phillips Brothers
- 2 tablespoons olive oil

Preheat the oven to 300°F. Place a baking rack with a tightly woven grid over a rimmed baking sheet and set aside. In a small bowl combine the granulated sugar, brown sugar, salt, cinnamon, and cayenne pepper, making sure there are no lumps; set aside.

Brush the ham slices on both sides with 1 tablespoon of the olive oil. Slice into small (approximately ⅓-inch) squares and toss in the remaining oil to make sure all surfaces are covered. Sprinkle with the sugar mixture and toss until evenly coated. Place the sugared ham on the rack and bake until the ham is caramelized and the sugar is bubbly, 30 to 40 minutes. Remove from the oven and cool completely (at least 30 minutes), separating the ham pieces as they cool. Store in a tightly sealed container until ready to eat.

BUTTERMILK FRIED CHICKEN

SERVES 4-6

FOR THE BRINE

- 5 lemons, halved
- 24 bay leaves
- 1 bunch (4 ounces) fresh flat-leaf parsley
- 1 bunch (1 ounce) fresh thyme
- ½ cup clover honey
- 1 head garlic, halved through the equator
- ¾ cup black peppercorns
- 2 cups (10 ounces) kosher salt, preferably Diamond Crystal
- 2 gallons water

- 2 2½- to 3-pound chickens (see Note on Chicken Size)

FOR DREDGING AND FRYING

- Peanut or canola oil, for deep-frying
- 1 quart buttermilk
- Kosher salt and freshly ground black pepper

FOR THE COATING

- 6 cups all-purpose flour
- ¼ cup garlic powder
- ¼ cup onion powder
- 1 tablespoon plus 1 teaspoon paprika
- 1 tablespoon plus 1 teaspoon cayenne
- 1 tablespoon plus 1 teaspoon kosher salt
- 1 teaspoon freshly ground black pepper

- Ground fleur de sel or fine sea salt
- Rosemary and thyme sprigs for garnish

He may be known as one of the world's most celebrated chefs, but these days my friend Thomas Keller is equally beloved for the fried chicken he serves at Ad Hoc, his bistro in Yountville, California. The herb-lemon brine helps keep the meat moist, and a double dip in seasoned flour between a buttermilk bath creates a feathery, crispy crust.

ON CHICKEN SIZE: *You may need to go to a farmers' market to get these small chickens. Grocery store chickens often run 3 to 4 pounds. They can, of course, be used in this recipe but if chickens in the 2½- to 3-pound range are available to you, they're worth seeking out. They're a little easier to cook properly at the temperatures we recommend here and, most important, pieces this size result in the optimal meat-to-crust proportion, which is such an important part of the pleasure of fried chicken.*

Combine all the brine ingredients in a large pot, cover, and bring to a boil. Boil for 1 minute, stirring to dissolve the salt. Remove from the heat and cool completely, then chill before using. The brine can be refrigerated for up to 3 days.

Cut each chicken into 10 pieces: 2 legs, 2 thighs, 4 breast quarters, and 2 wings. Pour the brine into a container large enough to hold the chicken pieces, add the chicken, and refrigerate for 12 hours (no longer, or the chicken may become too salty).

Remove the chicken from the brine (discard the brine) and rinse under cold water, removing any herbs or spices sticking to the skin. Pat dry with paper towels, or let air-dry. Let rest at room temperature for 1½ hours, or until it comes to room temperature.

If you have two large pots (about 6 inches deep) and a lot of oil, you can cook the dark and white meat at the same time; if not, cook the dark meat first, then turn up the heat and cook the white meat. No matter what size pot you have, the oil should not come more than one-third of the way up the sides of the pot. Fill the pot with at least 2 inches of peanut oil and heat to 320°F. Set a cooling rack over a baking sheet. Line a second baking sheet with parchment paper.

Meanwhile combine all the coating ingredients in a large bowl. Transfer half the coating to a second large bowl. Pour the buttermilk into a third bowl and season with salt and pepper. Set up a dipping station: the chicken pieces, one bowl of coating, the bowl of buttermilk, the second bowl of coating, and the parchment-lined baking sheet.

Just before frying, dip the chicken thighs into the first bowl of coating, turning to coat and patting off the excess; dip them into the buttermilk, allowing the excess to run back into the bowl; then dip them into the second bowl of coating. Transfer to the parchment-lined pan.

Carefully lower the thighs into the hot oil. Adjust the heat as necessary to return the oil to the proper temperature. Fry for 2 minutes, then carefully move the chicken pieces around in the oil and continue to fry, monitoring the oil temperature and turning the pieces as necessary for even cooking, for 11 to 12 minutes, until the chicken is a deep golden brown, cooked through, and very crisp. Meanwhile, coat the chicken drumsticks and transfer to the parchment-lined baking sheet.

Transfer the cooked thighs to the cooling rack skin side up and let rest while you fry the remaining chicken. (Putting the pieces skin side up will allow excess fat to drain, whereas leaving them skin side down could trap some of the fat.) Make sure that the oil is at the correct temperature, and cook the chicken drumsticks. When the drumsticks are done, lean them meat side up against the thighs to drain, then sprinkle the chicken with fine sea salt.

Turn up the heat and heat the oil to 340°F. Meanwhile, coat the chicken breasts and wings. Carefully lower the chicken breasts into the hot oil and fry for 7 minutes, or until golden brown, cooked through, and crisp. Transfer to the rack, sprinkle with salt, and turn skin side up. Cook the wings for 6 minutes, or until golden brown and cooked through. Transfer the wings to the rack and turn off the heat.

Arrange the chicken on a serving platter. Add the herb sprigs to the oil (which will still be hot) and let them cook and crisp for a few seconds, then arrange them over the chicken.

We let the chicken rest for 7 to 10 minutes after it comes out of the fryer so that it has a chance to cool down. If the chicken has rested for longer than 10 minutes, put the tray of chicken in a 400°F oven for a minute or two to ensure that the crust is crisp and the chicken is hot.

VENESSA WILLIAMS

CAJUN MOON FUNKY FRIED CHICKEN
and New Orleans–Style Vegetarian Red Beans and Rice

SERVES 4

Peanut oil, for frying
1 whole chicken, cut into 8 pieces and chilled
2 teaspoons kosher salt
1 tablespoon cayenne pepper
1½ cups all-purpose flour
1 large egg, beaten

Not just anyone gets the honor of feeding Mardi Gras's fiercest krewe, but New Orleans caterer Venessa Williams, a lifetime Louisiana resident and accomplished singer who sometimes performs with Kermit Ruffins (see page 92), is one of the lucky few. Commissioned yearly to feed the crowd at the Zulu Social Aide and Pleasure Club's annual parade party, she prepares thousands of pieces of her famous bird in giant, mobile, jerry-rigged fryers she designed herself. That chicken—accompanied by her tender, beautifully seasoned (and totally vegetarian) red beans and rice—have made her the go-to girl for church suppers, funerals, and Super Bowl parties alike. Williams's subtly spicy chicken is easy to replicate at home. She insists on using chilled chicken parts, an essential step for developing the crispest crust possible. That, and something a bit more intangible. "It's all about the vibrations," she trilled as she made us a batch in her kitchen, a tableful of ornate crucifixes stationed not ten feet away. Frying the cayenne-seasoned chicken in a stockpot filled halfway with oil, she watched as the chicken bobbed up and down in perfect pitch with its maker. "Keep it harmonious, and the chicken will follow," she said.

SEASON THE CHICKEN: Fill a large (at least 6-quart) pot halfway with the peanut oil and heat to 350°F. In a large bowl, toss the chicken with 1 teaspoon each of the salt and cayenne pepper.

DREDGE THE CHICKEN: In another large bowl, whisk the remaining teaspoon salt and 2 teaspoons cayenne pepper with the flour. Place the beaten egg in a third bowl, then toss the chicken in the egg. Working in batches of no more than 4 pieces at a time, toss the chicken in the flour mixture.

FRY THE CHICKEN: Fry the pieces in batches in the hot oil until cooked through, about 13 minutes for the breasts and 15 minutes for the thighs. Drain on a rack and serve immediately.

Venessa Williams at home with Lee Schrager; Venessa's chicken coming out of the frying pot

NEW ORLEANS–STYLE VEGETARIAN RED BEANS AND RICE

SERVES 8 GENEROUSLY

This is a meatless version of a beloved local classic. Red beans and rice are typically served at the beginning of the week in New Orleans, since Mondays were traditionally dedicated to the labor-intensive task of laundry, domestic workers prepared long-simmering stovetop dishes that required little attention. Camellia brand red beans, easily ordered online, are the classic choice for local New Orleans chefs, but any brand of kidney beans works fine; leaving the beans unsalted during cooking allows them to cook up faster and more tender.

1	pound dried Camellia brand red beans or red kidney beans
1	large onion, chopped
½	green bell pepper, chopped
½	red bell pepper, chopped
½	bunch fresh parsley, chopped
1	celery stalk, chopped
1	small habanero pepper, seeded (optional) and chopped
3	garlic cloves, chopped
2	teaspoons chopped fresh rosemary, or 1 teaspoon dried
2	teaspoons chopped fresh oregano, or 1 teaspoon dried
¼	cup olive oil
1	teaspoon sea salt, or more to taste
	Cooked rice, for serving (about 6 cups for a full batch)

Rinse and drain the beans three times and transfer to a large (at least 8-quart) saucepan with a lid. Add 7 cups water and all of the ingredients except the rice. Bring the beans to a boil, then cover tightly, reduce the heat to medium, and let cook, stirring once after about an hour, until they are tender and the liquid has thickened, 2 to 2½ hours. Remove from the heat and season with salt. Serve the beans over the cooked rice.

FRIED CHICKEN AND TOMATO PIE

CHICKEN SERVES 4; TOMATO PIE SERVES 8-10

1 whole chicken, cut into 8 pieces, giblets reserved if possible

2 teaspoons sea salt

1 teaspoon freshly ground black pepper

¾ cup buttermilk

2 cups all-purpose flour

½ teaspoon freshly ground white pepper

1 cup peanut oil

In Atlanta, a "tea room" isn't a place for finger sandwiches and Earl Grey, but rather a traditional "meat-and-three" dressed up just enough to suit occasions ranging from a workaday lunch to a family celebration. There used to be sixteen such establishments in Atlanta, but now there's only one: Mary Mac's. Originally opened in 1945, this warren of comfortable rooms serves a tasty combination of classic Southern food and Atlanta history. Photos of politicians, celebrities, and plain old patrons are featured alongside ephemera that tell the story of Mary Mac's three owners and those staff members who have been in the restaurant's employ for decades. The labyrinthine kitchen balances the high volume with a devotion to batch-by-batch quality. Mary Mac's chicken, fried and then steamed for optimum juiciness and crunch, has been on the menu since day one. The guilty-pleasure tomato pie is a more recent addition, now one of Mary Mac's most popular sides since being introduced a few years ago.

SEASON THE CHICKEN: Rinse the chicken and pat dry with paper towels. Sprinkle with 1 teaspoon of the salt and the black pepper; let stand for 15 minutes.

BATTER THE CHICKEN: Place the buttermilk in a medium bowl. In another bowl, whisk together the flour with the remaining 1 teaspoon salt and the white pepper. In a large (12-inch) cast-iron skillet with a lid, heat the oil to 375°F (very hot but not smoking). Working one piece at a time, dip the chicken in the buttermilk, then in the flour mixture, reserving on a tray until ready to fry.

FRY THE CHICKEN: Place the larger pieces of chicken in the pan, skin side down, then fit the smaller pieces around them, making sure as much of the surface of the chicken as possible is touching the skillet directly. Cover, reduce the heat to medium-high, and cook until the underside is browned and crisp, 9 to 10 minutes. Uncover, flip the chicken, add the giblets (if available), then cover and cook until the second side is browned and crisp, 9 to 10 minutes. Uncover and carefully add 1 cup water to the skillet in a slow stream, cover, and cook an additional 5 minutes. Drain on paper towels and serve warm.

A cook at Mary Mac's with a platter of their iconic fried chicken.

A feast of Mary Mac's Tea Room's Fried Chicken and Tomato Pie

TOMATO PIE

SERVES 8 TO 10

2 tablespoons olive oil, plus more for greasing
2 medium onions, very thinly sliced
   Kosher salt and freshly ground black pepper to taste
2 sleeves Ritz crackers, crushed by hand or in a
   food processor (about 2½ cups crushed)
2 28-ounce cans diced tomatoes in juice
2 cups mayonnaise
1½ cups (6 ounces) grated extra-sharp Cheddar cheese
1 cup freshly grated Parmigiano-Reggiano
   (or domestic Parmesan cheese)
2 tablespoons chopped fresh basil

Preheat the oven to 350°F. Grease a 9 × 13-inch oval baking dish with oil and set aside.

In a large skillet, heat the oil over medium heat. Add the onions and cook, stirring, until soft and translucent, 8 to 9 minutes. Season generously with salt and pepper and set aside. Scatter 1 cup cracker crumbs in the bottom of the baking dish. Pour 1 can tomatoes, juice included, over the crackers. Layer half the onions on top of the tomatoes; repeat the layering with the remaining can of tomatoes and onions. Sprinkle 1 cup cracker crumbs over the top onion layer.

In a medium bowl, combine the mayonnaise, Cheddar, Parmigiano-Reggiano, and basil. Spread over the top of the layers and top with the remaining ½ cup cracker crumbs. Bake the pie until golden brown, 35 to 40 minutes.

WHEN CHEF SCOTT PEACOCK *first turned to Edna Lewis for cooking advice in the early days of his career, he had no way of predicting how the aging African American legend of Southern cooking would change his life. Lewis saw in Peacock an unconventional kindred spirit, eventually anointing him the keeper of a treasured culinary canon that fused her cooking prowess with decades of experience. Together they wrote a cookbook, The Gift of Southern Cooking, and Peacock became Lewis's caretaker in the years before her death in 2006. Among the many legacies she left him was her fried chicken recipe, which Peacock was able to share with a generation of diners as the longtime chef and co-owner of Atlanta's Watershed restaurant (Peacock is no longer associated with the restaurant). "The thing that was so radical was that fat blend," said Peacock of the trinity of butter, lard, and rendered country ham that imparts Southern flavor in every bite. Over time Peacock also discovered that he preferred a mere hint of coating, which he refers to as a "rumor" of flour.*

SCOTT PEACOCK

EDNA'S FRIED CHICKEN
and Classic Buttermilk Biscuits

SERVES 4

FOR THE BRINE

- ½ cup kosher salt (do not use table salt for brining)
- 1 whole chicken, cut into 8 pieces
- 1 quart buttermilk

FOR FRYING

- 1 pound (2 cups) lard (see page 21)
- ½ cup (1 stick) unsalted butter
- ½ cup country ham pieces, or 1 thick slice country ham cut into ½-inch strips
- 1 cup all-purpose flour
- 2 tablespoons cornstarch
- 1 teaspoon kosher salt
- ½ teaspoon freshly ground black pepper

BRINE THE CHICKEN: In a large nonreactive bowl or pot, combine the salt with 2 quarts cold water. Add the chicken, cover, and refrigerate for 8 to 12 hours. Drain the chicken, rinse out the brining bowl, return the chicken to the bowl, and cover with the buttermilk. Cover and refrigerate for 8 to 12 hours. Remove the chicken from the buttermilk, transfer to a wire rack, and drain.

FRY THE CHICKEN: In a heavy 10- or 12-inch skillet or frying pan, combine the lard, butter, and ham. Cook over low heat for 30 to 45 minutes, skimming as needed, until the butter ceases to throw off foam and the ham is browned. Using a slotted spoon, carefully remove the ham from the fat and discard. Heat the fat to 335°F on a deep-fry thermometer.

DREDGE THE CHICKEN: In a shallow bowl or on a large piece of wax paper, blend together the flour, cornstarch, salt, and pepper. Dredge the drained chicken thoroughly in the flour mixture, then pat well to remove all excess flour.

FRY THE CHICKEN: Using tongs and working in batches, place half of the chicken, skin side down, into the heated fat. Regulate the fat so it just bubbles, and cook until the chicken is golden brown and cooked through, 8 to 10 minutes on each side. Drain thoroughly on a wire rack or on crumpled paper towels and serve.

CLASSIC BUTTERMILK BISCUITS
MAKES 12 BISCUITS

These light-as-air biscuits are considered the gold standard. Serve them warm, with butter or honey or—better yet—both. Peacock makes his own baking powder mix of cream of tartar and baking soda, but if you're in a hurry, simply replace with 1½ tablespoons store-bought baking powder.

  5 cups sifted unbleached all-purpose flour (about 1¼ pounds, measured after sifting), plus more for rolling
  1 tablespoon cream of tartar
1½ teaspoons baking soda
  1 tablespoon kosher salt
  ½ cup plus 2 tablespoons packed lard or unsalted butter, chilled
  2 cups chilled buttermilk, plus more as needed
  3 tablespoons unsalted butter, melted

Arrange the oven rack in the upper third of the oven and preheat the oven to 500°F. In a large bowl, whisk together the flour, cream of tartar, baking soda, and salt. Add the lard in one large piece, coating it in the flour. Working quickly, rub the lard briskly between your fingertips (or use a pastry blender) until roughly half the lard is coarsely blended and half remains in large, ¾-inch pieces. Form a well in the center of the flour mixture and add the buttermilk all at once. With a large spoon, stir the mixture quickly until just blended and a sticky mass of dough is formed, adding 1 to 2 tablespoons additional buttermilk if necessary.

Transfer the dough to a generously floured surface. Using floured hands, very gently knead until a cohesive ball of dough forms, 8 to 10 times. Gently flatten the dough and then, using a floured rolling pin, lightly roll the dough ¾ inch thick. Dip a fork in flour and pierce the dough through to the surface at ½-inch intervals. Using a floured 2½- or 3-inch biscuit cutter, cut out rounds and arrange on a heavy parchment-lined baking sheet. Do not reroll the dough, but add the leftover dough to the baking sheet. Bake until the tops are crusty and golden brown, 9 to 11 minutes. Remove from the oven, brush with melted butter, and serve hot.

MIKE MOORE

SEVEN SOWS FRIED CHICKEN
with Egg and Giblet Gravy, and Macaroni and Cheese

SERVES 4, PLUS EXTRA MACARONI AND CHEESE

FOR THE BUTTERMILK BRINE AND BATTER

- 2 cups buttermilk, preferably Cruze Dairy brand (available primarily in the South)
- 1 cup hot sauce, preferably Texas Pete's
- 3 sprigs fresh thyme
- 4 garlic cloves, peeled and smashed
- 1 whole chicken, cut into 8 pieces

FOR THE DREDGE

- 2 cups all-purpose flour
- 2 tablespoons paprika
- 2 tablespoons salt
- 2 teaspoons freshly ground black pepper
- 1 teaspoon onion powder
- 1 teaspoon garlic powder
- 1 teaspoon dried thyme

  Peanut oil, for frying

FOR THE GRAVY

- 4 tablespoons unsalted butter
- 2 chicken gizzards
- 1 chicken neck bone
- 1 chicken liver
- ½ small onion, finely diced
- 2 garlic cloves, minced
- ¼ cup all-purpose flour
- ½ teaspoon chopped fresh thyme leaves
- ½ teaspoon kosher salt
- ¼ teaspoon freshly ground black pepper
- 3 cups low-sodium chicken stock, plus more as needed

I'm a sucker for gravy, and Chef Mike Moore at Seven Sows Bourbon & Larder in Asheville, North Carolina, makes a great, soulful one from often-neglected parts of the chicken, inspired by gravy he grew up on courtesy of his grandma Carlie, a farmer's wife from Wilson, North Carolina. In the tradition of Southern recipes, this one with its use of oft-discarded chicken parts has its roots in the "waste not, want not" school of cooking. For special occasions Carlie would add a slice of pimento on top of her chicken to dress up the plate, so naturally that's what Chef Mike does, too. "I opened a restaurant with a pig in the name, and lo and behold our most popular menu item is the fried chicken," says Moore. The super-rich macaroni and cheese, based on a classic Mornay sauce, gilds the lily here.

BRINE THE CHICKEN: Combine the buttermilk, hot sauce, thyme sprigs, and garlic in a large bowl or resealable container. Add the chicken pieces, toss to coat, cover, and refrigerate for 48 hours.

MAKE THE DREDGE: In a large bowl, combine the flour, paprika, salt, pepper, onion powder, garlic powder, and thyme.

FRY THE CHICKEN: Heat a large pot filled halfway with oil to 350°F. Remove the chicken from the brine and allow the excess to drip off for about 5 seconds. Using your hands, toss the chicken in the flour dredge. Working in batches, fry the chicken until it is brown and crispy and the internal temperature reaches 165°F, 13 to 15 minutes. Drain on paper towels.

MAKE THE GRAVY: While the chicken is frying, heat the butter in a large skillet over medium heat. Add the gizzards, neck bone, and liver and sauté until the meat has browned, 4 to 5 minutes. Add the onion and cook until translucent, 4 to 5 minutes. Lower heat slightly, then add the garlic and cook 1 additional minute. Add the flour, thyme, salt, and pepper and cook, stirring, until the mixture

1 large hard-boiled egg, chopped
1 small jar sliced pimento (roasted red pepper) strips, drained and rinsed

has thickened, 2 to 3 minutes. Raise heat to medium, then add the chicken stock and cook, stirring, until the mixture thickens to a gravy-like consistency, 4 to 5 minutes, adding additional stock by the tablespoonful to thin out the gravy if necessary. Season again with salt and pepper to taste. Remove and discard the neck bone, gizzards, and livers.

TO SERVE: Arrange the chicken on a platter and top with the gravy, hard-boiled egg, and pimento strips. Serve with the macaroni and cheese.

MACARONI AND CHEESE

½ small red onion, peeled
1 bay leaf
3 cloves
5 tablespoons unsalted butter
5 tablespoons all-purpose flour
2 cups heavy cream
1 cup whole milk
2 tablespoons dry white wine
1 tablespoon fresh thyme leaves
   Kosher salt and freshly ground black pepper to taste
2 cups (8 ounces) roughly grated white Cheddar cheese
1 pound macaroni, cooked according to package directions
1 teaspoon lemon zest

An onion piqué (French for "pricked onion") is a clove- and bay leaf–studded onion used to subtly flavor dishes with a hint of warm and piney spices.

To make an onion piqué (see Note), affix the bay leaf to the cut sides of the red onion by piercing with the cloves; reserve. In a medium saucepan heat the butter over medium-high heat. Add the flour all at once and cook, stirring, until lightly browned, 6 to 7 minutes. Add the cream, milk, wine, thyme, onion piqué, salt, and pepper. Cook over low heat, stirring, for 10 minutes, until slightly thickened. Remove and discard the onion piqué and strain the mixture through a fine strainer into a bowl. Return the strained mixture to a skillet set over medium heat; stir in the cheese and cook until thick and creamy, 2 to 3 minutes. Fold in the cooked macaroni and lemon zest; season with more salt and pepper.

FRIED CHICKEN *and* SWISS CHARD SALAD
with Pine Nuts and Lemon

SERVES 4

FOR THE SPICE MIX

- 2 tablespoons paprika
- 1 tablespoon cayenne pepper
- 1 teaspoon smoked paprika
- 1 teaspoon dried thyme
- 1 teaspoon dried oregano
- 1 teaspoon garlic powder
- 1 teaspoon onion powder
- 1 teaspoon freshly ground black pepper

FOR THE CHICKEN

- 2 cups buttermilk
- 2 tablespoons kosher salt
- 4 bone-in, skin-on chicken thighs
- 4 bone-in, skin-on chicken drumsticks
- 4 cups vegetable oil, for frying
- 2 cups self-rising flour

I can't remember the first time I met Art Smith, but I can vividly recall the first time I tasted the fried chicken at his Chicago restaurant, Table 52. Each bite was incredibly crunchy due to a long fry at a low temperature, and from that night on I vowed to schedule my trips to the Windy City to coincide with the nights he fried chicken at his restaurant. One taste of his chicken and lemony Swiss chard salad, and you'll see why Oprah kept him all to herself—as her personal chef—for all those years. When Art makes his annual visit to my summer home, there's only one caveat: he must make a fried chicken dinner before he leaves. That annual beachside meal never fails to be anything short of spectacular.

MAKE THE SPICE MIX: In a small bowl, combine the paprika, cayenne pepper, smoked paprika, thyme, oregano, garlic powder, onion powder, and black pepper. Set aside.

BRINE THE CHICKEN: In a large bowl, whisk together the buttermilk, 1 tablespoon of the salt, and 2 tablespoons of the spice mix. Place all the chicken pieces in an airtight container or Ziploc bag. Pour the buttermilk mixture over the chicken, seal, and refrigerate for 24 to 48 hours.

FRY THE CHICKEN: In a large, high-sided skillet, slowly heat the oil to 325°F. Place the flour in a large bowl and stir in the remaining spice mix and the remaining 1 tablespoon of salt. Set a wire rack on top of a rimmed baking sheet and set aside. Remove the chicken from the buttermilk brine and dredge in the seasoned flour, shaking off the excess, then dredge again in the flour to form a double crust. Working in batches, gently place the chicken into the hot oil; the temperature will drop to 265°F to 275°F. Fry the chicken until deep brown and crisp, 12 to 14 minutes for the first side and 10 to 12 minutes for the other side. Transfer the fried pieces to the rack and let rest for 5 to 10 minutes before serving.

SWISS CHARD SALAD WITH PINE NUTS AND LEMON

SERVES 4

8 large Swiss chard leaves (about ¾ pound), trimmed and thinly shredded crosswise

¼ cup extra-virgin olive oil

2 tablespoons freshly squeezed lemon juice

¼ cup freshly grated Parmigiano-Reggiano, or more to taste

¼ cup lightly toasted pine nuts

Kosher salt and freshly ground black pepper to taste

In a medium bowl, toss the chard, oil, and lemon juice. Add the cheese and pine nuts and toss to incorporate. Season with salt and pepper to taste.

JACQUES PÉPIN

FRIED CHICKEN SOUTHERN-STYLE
with Corn Bread Sticks

SERVES 4

1 whole chicken, cut into 8 pieces
1 cup buttermilk
1 teaspoon kosher salt
1 teaspoon Tabasco sauce,
   or to taste
2 cups lard
2 cups peanut oil
1 cup all-purpose flour
1 teaspoon baking powder
   Corn on the cob and buttered
   baguettes for serving

One of my favorite memories of all time remains the Friday night all-you-can-eat fried chicken buffet at Howard Johnson's. The buffet included mountains of juicy, crunchy fried chicken (my personal record was fourteen pieces). Many years later, as a culinary student, I learned that one of my heroes, Jacques Pépin, had been Howard Johnson's test-kitchen research director for a decade and had had a hand in creating that fried chicken recipe. Growing up near Lyons, France, and even serving as personal chef to French heads of state, Pépin hardly knew fried chicken existed. "We did poulet ten different ways—even in a skillet with butter and oil—but we really never breaded and fried." That all changed soon after he moved to New York in the late 1950s to work at the famed Le Pavillon, at the time one of the city's finest restaurants. One of the regular patrons was none other than Howard Johnson, the chain's founder. Johnson recruited Pépin and fellow Frenchman Pierre Franey to bring a fresh, yet classically trained, eye to every dish. Before his arrival, HoJo's fried chicken was prepared with cracker meal and evaporated milk; Pépin introduced half-and-half, buttermilk, and fresh bread crumbs, then sifted baking powder into the dredge to create the bird's crackery crust. Their signature recipe was enjoyed by generations of Howard Johnson's patrons, and though there remains only one Howard Johnson's restaurant, in Lake Placid, New York, a version of fried chicken is still on the menu.

SEASON THE CHICKEN: Place the chicken in a Ziploc bag, then add the buttermilk, salt, and Tabasco sauce. Seal and shake to evenly distribute the buttermilk and seasonings. Refrigerate for at least 2 hours or overnight.

DREDGE THE CHICKEN: In a 12-inch skillet with a tight-fitting lid, gently heat the lard and oil to 350°F. Set a wire rack over a rimmed baking sheet. In a large bowl, combine the flour and baking powder. Remove the chicken pieces from the buttermilk mixture, keeping as much as of the buttermilk coating on the pieces as possible. Dredge the chicken in the flour mixture until thickly covered on all sides.

FRY THE CHICKEN: Place the chicken, skin side down, in the hot oil; the oil should be deep enough so that it comes almost to the top of the chicken pieces. Cover tightly, reduce the heat to medium-low, and cook until the exterior is deeply browned and crisp, 17 to 19 minutes. Transfer the chicken to the rack to cool. (The chicken can be kept warm in a 170°F oven for 1 hour.)

TO SERVE: Serve the chicken and corn bread sticks with hot corn on the cob and buttered crusty baguettes.

CORN BREAD STICKS

MAKES 7 STICKS

If you don't have the cornstick mold, this recipe makes 12 corn muffins; bake for the same time and at the same temperature.

- 1 cup yellow cornmeal
- ½ cup all-purpose flour
- ½ teaspoon baking powder or baking soda (either works here)
- ¾ teaspoon kosher salt
- 2 tablespoons sugar
- ½ cup whole milk
- ½ cup buttermilk
- 6 tablespoons unsalted butter, melted
- 2 large eggs, yolks and whites separated
- 1 tablespoon peanut or corn oil

Special Equipment: a 7-compartment cast-iron cornstick mold (available online)

Preheat the oven to 425°F. In a medium bowl, whisk together the cornmeal, flour, baking powder, salt, and sugar. Whisk in the milk, buttermilk, butter, and egg yolks until smooth. Generously grease the indentations in a cornstick mold with the oil, place on a cookie sheet, and heat in the oven for 5 minutes.

In a medium bowl, beat the egg whites until they are just frothy. Fold into the batter until just combined. Remove the heated mold from the oven and spoon the batter into the hot mold. Return the mold to the oven and bake until puffy and brown, 20 to 22 minutes. Cool, unmold, and serve warm with butter.

ANDREW CARMELLINI

THE DUTCH'S FRIED CHICKEN

SERVES 4

FOR THE BUTTERMILK MARINADE

- 4 cups buttermilk
- 2 tablespoons honey
- 2 teaspoons Old Bay seasoning
- 2 teaspoons kosher salt
- 2 teaspoons Tabasco sauce
- 1 teaspoon freshly ground black pepper
- ¼ teaspoon cayenne pepper
- 2 whole chickens (about 3 pounds each), cut into desired pieces

- 8 cups corn oil

FOR THE DREDGE

- 4 teaspoons paprika
- 1 tablespoon kosher salt
- 2 teaspoons chili powder
- 2 teaspoons garlic powder
- 2 teaspoons onion powder
- 2 tablespoons Old Bay seasoning
- 2 teaspoons cayenne pepper
- 2 teaspoons ground celery seed
- 1 teaspoon freshly ground black pepper
- 4 cups all-purpose flour

A few years back, Andrew Carmellini began holding sold-out fried chicken dinners, thrown at his New York restaurant, Locanda Verde. They were so popular that he gave his crunchy, aggressively spiced bird a regular spot on the menu for The Dutch, which has locations in SoHo and Miami. So devoted to fried chicken is Andrew that he now hosts the Chicken Coupe fried chicken event at the Food Network South Beach Wine & Food Festival.

MARINATE THE CHICKEN: In a large mixing bowl, whisk together the buttermilk, honey, Old Bay, salt, Tabasco sauce, black pepper, and cayenne pepper. Place the chicken in the marinade, cover, and refrigerate for 12 hours. Remove the chicken from the refrigerator and bring to room temperature for 1 hour.

MAKE THE FLOUR DREDGE: Preheat the oven to 200°F. Heat 3 inches oil in a deep pot to 350°F, until the oil starts to pop. While the oil is heating, in a large bowl whisk together the paprika, salt, chili powder, garlic powder, onion powder, Old Bay, cayenne pepper, celery seed, and black pepper. Remove half the spice mixture (about ¾ cup) to a separate small bowl. In the large bowl containing half the spice mix, whisk in the flour until incorporated.

FRY THE CHICKEN: When the oil is hot, remove a chicken piece from the marinade and toss in the flour mixture until coated. Repeat with the remaining pieces until there is no more space in the bowl. Set a wire rack over a baking sheet and set aside. Working in batches, remove each chicken piece from the flour, give it a light shake, and place it in the oil. Fry until golden brown, about 9 minutes. Remove the chicken from the oil, place on the wire rack, and sprinkle on all sides with the remaining spice mix.

BAKE THE CHICKEN: Place the chicken pieces in the oven to rest for at least 10 minutes, to allow the cooking process to finish. Keep the chicken in the oven until all the pieces are fried and finished in the oven. Serve hot.

Andrew Carmellini's Fried Chicken

BEST EVER SOUTHERN FRIED CHICKEN

SERVES 4

- 3 large eggs
- 2 cups self-rising flour
- 1 teaspoon freshly ground black pepper, plus more for seasoning
- 1 small whole chicken (up to 2½ pounds), washed, patted dry, and cut into 10 pieces
  Sea salt
- 4 cups solid vegetable shortening, such as Crisco, for deep-frying

Before I met Paula Deen in person, I fell in love with the heavenly fried chicken she served at The Lady & Sons, her Savannah restaurant. Looking at the long line of people waiting outside the front door, I wondered what all the fuss was about . . . then understood after just one bite why Paula was—and is—the reigning queen of Southern cooking. It was her fried chicken—simply dipped, dredged, and fried—that first caught my eye. The combination of eggs and self-rising flour promises extra-airy, crispy results that will be the star of your next dinner party or picnic. Make sure to use a very small chicken, or increase the frying time accordingly.

MAKE THE DREDGE: In a shallow bowl, lightly beat the eggs with ⅓ cup water. In a separate shallow bowl, combine the flour and pepper. Set aside.

DREDGE THE CHICKEN: Lightly season the chicken all over with salt and pepper. Dip the chicken pieces in the egg mixture, letting any excess drip off, and then coat well in the flour mixture.

FRY THE CHICKEN: In a large (at least 12-inch), high-sided skillet, heat the shortening to 350°F until it has melted to a liquid 2 inches deep in the skillet. Slip the chicken into the melted fat (the fat should just come up over the chicken) and cook the pieces in batches until browned and crisp, 13 to 14 minutes for the dark meat and 9 to 10 minutes for the white meat. Drain on paper towels and serve warm or at room temperature.

MARTHA LOU'S FRIED CHICKEN

SERVES 4

FOR THE SEASONING

- 1 whole chicken, cut into quarters
- 1½ teaspoons kosher salt
- ½ teaspoon freshly ground black pepper
- 1 teaspoon seasoning salt, such as Accent

FOR FRYING

- 2 cups whole milk
- 2 cups self-rising flour
- ½ teaspoon kosher salt
  Peanut oil, for frying

When we asked Martha Lou Gadsden, of Martha Lou's Kitchen in Charleston, South Carolina, why people came from near and far for her fried chicken, she was quick with an answer. "I fry to order because I don't like the cooked bird sitting up there all by itself," she said. "So my chicken's always fresh." Martha Lou started out in the restaurant business by helping at a friend's place, long before she struck out on her own. "I've been in business since 1983 and now I am eighty-three," said Martha Lou. "You learn by doing, and now I've been doing this for a long time. At that rate, you get progress." Her recipe may be exceedingly simple, but there's an ingenious butchering twist that sets Martha Lou's process apart from the coop: strategic cuts in the meat that help the chicken cook evenly and efficiently. A slit through the middle of the breast quarter, and another at the joint between the leg and the thigh, speed up the cooking process and eliminate the rivulet of red "chicken juice" Ms. Gadsden finds distasteful.

SEASON THE CHICKEN: Rinse the chicken and thoroughly pat dry with paper towels. Using a sharp knife, make a slit in the center of each breast quarter, as though preparing the breast for stuffing. Make a slit in the leg quarter at the joint, making sure not to cut so far as to separate the leg from the thigh. Season the chicken pieces (including the breast cavities) thoroughly with salt, pepper, and seasoning salt. Place in a Ziploc bag or bowl, seal, and refrigerate for 2 to 3 hours or overnight.

PREPARE THE DIP AND DREDGE: Place the milk in a bowl. In a separate bowl, whisk together the flour and salt.

DREDGE AND FRY THE CHICKEN: Prepare a deep-fryer or a large (at least 6-quart) pot filled hallway with oil and heat to 350°F. Dip the chicken in the milk, shaking off the excess, then in the seasoned flour. Working in batches, fry the chicken until cooked through, 16 to 17 minutes for the leg quarters and 15 minutes for the breast quarters. Drain on paper towels and serve hot.

AMERICAN ORIGINALS

IN HIS BOOK *Fried Chicken: An American Story*, food authority John T. Edge aimed to demonstrate that fried chicken was a wholly American art form rather than merely a Southern one—a generous admission from the man whose Southern Foodways Alliance works to preserve food traditions below the Mason-Dixon line. "For decades fried chicken was slumbering in the Southern ghetto, and now it has emerged," he told us. "Chefs and consumers have embraced it in a way that celebrates its Southern-ness but brings all sorts of ethnicities and regional specialties to bear." We couldn't agree more, and this collection of recipes only bolsters the argument. Some contain heavy Southern influences, but their accompanying side dishes modernize both presentation and experience. Still others beautifully reflect the influence of immigration and the way it creates new traditions that get stirred up in the American melting pot. When it comes to fried chicken it's hard to say where the South ends and the rest of America begins, but one thing's for sure: as a group these recipes are proof positive that fried chicken can hold its own in any state—and any style—of the union.

OPPOSITE: Café Boulud's Skinless Fried Chicken, Baked Beans, and Pickled Fresno Chiles, see page 140 for recipe.

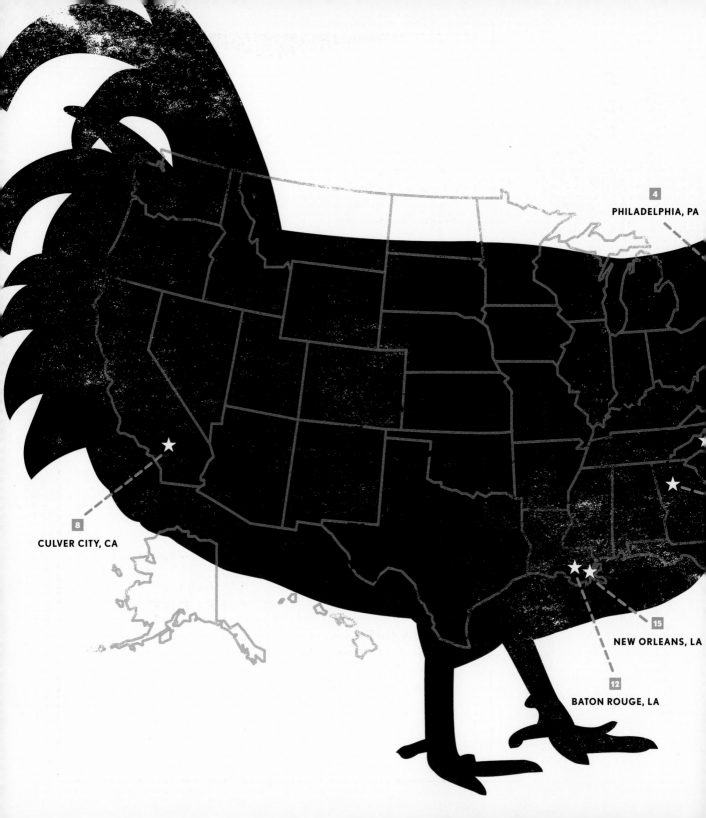

4 PHILADELPHIA, PA

8 CULVER CITY, CA

15 NEW ORLEANS, LA

12 BATON ROUGE, LA

1 **GAVIN KAYSEN**
Café Boulud's Skinless Fried Chicken, Baked Beans, and Pickled Fresno Chiles

2 **MICHELLE BERNSTEIN**
Michy's Fried Chicken and Watermelon Greek Salad

3 **BLACKBERRY FARM**
Sweet Tea–Brined Fried Chicken

4 **MICHAEL SOLOMONOV**
Federal Donuts Fried Chicken and Sauce

5 **WYLIE DUFRESNE**
Popeyes-Style Chicken Tenders and Biscuits

6 **ASHA GOMEZ**
Keralan Fried Chicken, Lowcountry Cardamom Waffles, and Spicy Maple Syrup

7 **MARCUS SAMUELSSON**
Coconut Fried Chicken with Collards and Gravy

8 **HONEY'S KETTLE**
Home-Style Smashed Garlic Fried Chicken

9 **HIGHLAND KITCHEN**
Fried (Chicken) and Frozen (Cocktail)

10 **MICHAEL ROMANO**
Graham Cracker–Crusted Chicken

11 **PARM**
Fried Chicken Cacciatore

12 **RUSTY HAMLIN**
Louisiana Battered Fried Chicken

13 **PIERRE THIAM**
Senegalese Fried Chicken

14 **STEVEN SATTERFIELD**
Yogurt-Marinated Chicken Thighs, Charred Vegetables, and Honey-Vinegar Glaze

15 **TUJAGUE'S**
Chicken Bonne Femme

16 **JEFF MCINNIS**
Fried Chicken and Cauliflower Mash

BOSTON, MA 9

HARLEM, NY 13 7

NEW YORK, NY 1 11 10

BROOKLYN, NY 16

ASHEVILLE, NC 3

ATLANTA, GA 6 14 5

MIAMI, FL 2

GAVIN KAYSEN

CAFÉ BOULUD'S SKINLESS FRIED CHICKEN,
Baked Beans and Barbecue Sauce, and Pickled Fresno Chiles

SERVES 4

FOR THE BRINE

- 1 cup kosher salt
- ½ cup honey
- 4 sprigs fresh thyme
- 3 sprigs fresh rosemary
- 2 garlic cloves, crushed
- 1 dried bay leaf
- 2 teaspoons black peppercorns
- 4 cups ice
- 1 whole chicken, completely skinned except for wings, cut into 10 pieces
- 4 cups buttermilk

FOR DREDGING AND FRYING

- 4 cups all-purpose flour
- 1 tablespoon baking powder
- ½ teaspoon cracked black pepper
- 1½ teaspoons paprika
- 1½ teaspoons onion powder
- 1½ teaspoons garlic powder
- 1½ tablespoons La Boîte à Épices kibbeh spice or Old Bay seasoning
- 4 cups vegetable oil
- 2 cups rendered duck fat or vegetable oil
  Additional fresh thyme and rosemary sprigs, for frying
  Additional garlic cloves, for frying

Located in one of Manhattan's toniest neighborhoods, Café Boulud empties out on summer weekends as its patrons retreat to cooler climes. To reward the regulars who stick around, Chef Gavin Kaysen puts fried chicken on the menu—and has been pleasantly surprised at how enthusiastically his clientele has embraced the dish. "Nothing makes me smile like seeing them enjoy beautiful bottles of French wine while tearing chicken apart with their hands," he said. Skinning the chicken and then air-drying the meat before frying ensures crispness and eliminates the danger of any unrendered fat lingering beneath the crust—it takes 36 hours before the bird even hits the pan, but it's worth the wait. The kibbeh spice blend, available online from la Boîte à Epices, is a heady mix of flavors typically used to season Middle Eastern ground beef patties, but Old Bay works well, too. The pickled Fresno chiles, so simple to prepare, cut through the chicken's richness and last for a month in the fridge—a good thing, since you'll want to put them on absolutely everything.

MAKE THE BRINE: In a large saucepan, combine the salt, honey, 2 thyme sprigs, 1 rosemary sprig, 1 garlic clove, the bay leaf, and 1 teaspoon peppercorns with 4 cups water. Bring to a boil, stirring until the honey has dissolved. Place the ice in a large bowl, then pour the hot liquid over the ice. Cool in the refrigerator for 1 hour.

BRINE THE CHICKEN: Place the chicken in a large bowl or resealable container. Pour the cooled brine over the chicken, then cover and refrigerate for 12 hours. Set a wire rack over a rimmed baking sheet and set aside. Rinse the chicken, transfer to the rack, and air-dry, uncovered, in the refrigerator for 12 hours. In a large bowl, combine the buttermilk with the remaining 2 thyme sprigs, 2 rosemary sprigs, 1 garlic clove, and 1 teaspoon peppercorns. Add the chicken to the bowl, toss, and refrigerate for 12 hours.

DREDGE THE CHICKEN: In a large bowl, whisk together the flour, baking powder, pepper, paprika, onion powder, garlic powder, and kibbeh spice. One piece at a time, remove the chicken from the buttermilk and dip directly into the flour mixture, then back into the buttermilk, then back into the flour, shaking off the excess at each stage. Set a wire rack over a rimmed baking sheet and set aside.

FRY THE CHICKEN: Preheat the oven to 375°F. Heat the oil and duck fat in a large (12- or 14-inch) cast-iron skillet to 350°F. Working in batches and frying a maximum of 5 pieces at a time, fry the chicken until golden brown, 5 to 6 minutes per side. Transfer the finished pieces to the rack and keep warm in the oven while frying the remainder of the chicken.

FRY THE HERBS: Submerge the additional thyme and rosemary sprigs and garlic cloves in the still-hot oil until the cloves are golden and the oil is fragrant, 2 to 3 minutes. Serve the chicken with the fried herbs and garlic, baked beans, and pickled chiles.

Save the chicken skins to make Sean Brock's Southern Fried Chicken Skins (page 226) or Kenny & Zuke's Gribenes Rillettes (page 229).

BAKED BEANS AND BARBECUE SAUCE

SERVES 6-8

FOR THE BEANS

1 pound (2 ½ cups) navy or other
   small white beans
2 tablespoons vegetable oil
1 medium onion, halved
1 medium carrot, quartered
1 celery stalk, halved
1 garlic clove, smashed
2 sprigs fresh thyme
1 sprig fresh rosemary
4 cups chicken stock

FOR THE SAUCE

3 tablespoons vegetable oil
1 large yellow onion, finely diced
½ red onion, finely diced
2 tablespoons (packed) light brown
   sugar
1 tablespoon yellow mustard powder
1 teaspoon onion powder
¼ teaspoon cayenne pepper
3 tablespoons cider vinegar
¾ cup ketchup
1 tablespoon Worcestershire sauce
1 teaspoon Tabasco sauce
1 dried bay leaf
2 sprigs fresh thyme
1 sprig fresh rosemary
1 tablespoon honey, plus more to taste
   Kosher salt and freshly ground black
   pepper to taste

Kaysen's baked beans, made with homemade barbecue sauce, are a treat worth the extra effort (but feel free to sub in 2½ to 3 cups store-bought sauce to save time).

SOAK THE BEANS: In a large bowl, cover the beans with 4 inches water, cover, and soak for 24 hours, until fully rehydrated.

COOK THE BEANS: Preheat the oven to 325°F. Drain the soaked beans and set aside. In a large oven-proof pot with a lid, heat the oil over medium-high heat and cook the onion, carrot, and celery until golden brown, 13 to 14 minutes. Add the garlic and cook for 1 minute more. Tie the thyme and rosemary with kitchen twine and add the herb bundle to the pot with the beans and stock. Bring the pot to a simmer, cover, and bake in the oven until tender, 35 to 40 minutes. Remove from the oven and strain the beans, draining off any remaining liquid. Remove and discard the carrot, onion, and celery.

MAKE THE SAUCE: In a medium saucepan, heat the oil over medium-high heat. Add the yellow onion and red onion and cook, stirring, until golden, 11 to 12 minutes. Add the brown sugar, mustard powder, onion powder, and cayenne pepper, stirring to incorporate. Add the vinegar and deglaze the pan, scraping up any bits on the bottom, 1 minute. Add the ketchup, Worcestershire sauce, Tabasco sauce, bay leaf, thyme, rosemary, honey, and ¼ cup water. Bring the sauce to a boil, reduce the heat to low, and simmer until thickened, 11 to 12 minutes, adding additional water by the tablespoonful to loosen if necessary. Remove and discard the bay leaf, rosemary, and thyme, then remove half the sauce and reserve for another use.

SAUCE THE BEANS: Add the beans to the sauce, cover, and return to the oven to cook until the beans have absorbed some sauce and are tender, 15 to 20 minutes. Season with additional honey, salt, and pepper to taste.

PICKLED FRESNO CHILES

MAKES 1 PINT

- ½ cup Champagne vinegar
- 3 tablespoons sugar
- 6 Fresno or Anaheim chiles, thinly sliced into rounds

In a small saucepan, bring the vinegar, sugar, and 1 cup water to a simmer and cook until the sugar dissolves, 3 to 4 minutes. Place the chiles in a small bowl. Pour the pickling liquid over the chiles, let cool, and transfer to a pint jar. Seal and chill until ready to use.

MICHELLE BERNSTEIN

MICHY'S FRIED CHICKEN
and Watermelon Greek Salad

SERVES 4

FOR THE BRINE

- 1 whole chicken, cut into 8 pieces
- ¼ cup sugar
- ¼ cup kosher salt
- 1 teaspoon black peppercorns
- 1 dried bay leaf
- 1 teaspoon celery seeds
- 1 teaspoon fennel seeds

FOR DREDGING AND FRYING

- Safflower, peanut, or grapeseed oil, for frying
- 2 cups buttermilk
- 3 tablespoons hot sauce, preferably Cholula brand
- 3 cups all-purpose flour
- 2 tablespoons Old Bay seasoning
- 1½ tablespoons kosher salt
- 1 tablespoon cayenne pepper
- 1 tablespoon paprika
- Honey, for serving

Whoever thought a Jewish girl from Argentina could produce one of the best takes on an American favorite? But Michy—as everyone affectionately refers to beloved Miami restaurateur Michelle Bernstein— does exactly that. On summer Wednesdays she serves an incredible all- you-can-eat fried chicken buffet—the chicken gilded with an impossibly crisp coating—that calls to mind my meals as a kid at our local Howard Johnson's. Michy herself is a dark-meat aficionado, so feel free to swap out the white meat with more thighs and legs. The cool, refreshing salad is almost an optical illusion, the tomatoes and watermelon mimicking one another until they hit the tongue.

BRINE THE CHICKEN: Place the chicken in a large nonreactive container or dish. In another bowl, stir 8 cups water with the sugar, salt, peppercorns, bay leaf, celery seeds, and fennel seeds. Pour the brine over the chicken, cover, and refrigerate for 24 hours. Drain the brine from the chicken and rinse and dry the meat completely with paper towels.

DREDGE THE CHICKEN: Fill a large (12-inch) skillet just under halfway with the oil and heat to 275°F. Set a wire rack on top of a rimmed baking sheet and set aside. In a baking dish or bowl, combine the buttermilk and hot sauce. In another dish, combine the flour, Old Bay, salt, cayenne pepper, and paprika. Dredge the chicken pieces in the flour mixture, shaking off the excess, then dip into the buttermilk mixture, then back into the flour mixture, shaking the dish to coat the chicken evenly.

FRY THE CHICKEN: Fry the chicken 4 pieces at a time until golden and fully cooked through, 8 to 9 minutes per side. Remove the chicken from the oil and drain on the rack; cool for 10 minutes. Heat the oil back up to 350°F. Refry the chicken in batches until it darkens and crisps, an additional 5 minutes. Remove from the oil and drain the chicken on the wire rack. Drizzle with honey.

WATERMELON GREEK SALAD

SERVES 4

1   1¾-pound wedge of watermelon, rind removed
    and cut into medium dice (about 4 cups)
2   large beefsteak tomatoes (1¼ pounds),
    seeded and cut into small dice (about 2 cups)
1   large English hothouse cucumber (¾ pound),
    peeled and cut into small dice (about 2 cups)
1   cup crumbled feta cheese
2   tablespoons torn dill, uncut
¼   cup extra-virgin olive oil
2   tablespoons red wine vinegar
    Pinch of garlic powder
    Pinch of onion powder
    Kosher salt and freshly ground black pepper
    to taste

In a large bowl, combine the watermelon, tomatoes, cucumber, feta, and dill. In a small bowl, whisk together the oil, vinegar, garlic powder, and onion powder; season with salt and pepper to taste. Drizzle half the vinaigrette over the salad and toss very gently. Add the remaining dressing to taste and gently toss again.

SWEET TEA–BRINED FRIED CHICKEN

SERVES 4

FOR THE BRINE

- 1 quart very strong brewed tea (made with a brand such as Lipton)
- 1 cup sugar
- ½ cup kosher salt
- 1 lemon, zested and quartered
- 8 bone-in, skin-on chicken legs and 8 chicken thighs

FOR THE DREDGE

- 4 cups all-purpose flour
- 2 cups masa harina
- 2 tablespoons Old Bay seasoning
- 1 tablespoon chili powder
- 1 teaspoon kosher salt, plus more to taste
- ¼ teaspoon freshly ground black pepper, plus more to taste

FOR THE BUTTERMILK DIP

- 4 large eggs
- ½ cup buttermilk

  Vegetable oil, for frying

When I visit my parents in Asheville, North Carolina, we usually take a day trip to Blackberry Farm, which is a gorgeous 2½-hour drive away and is known as much for its incredible food as its bucolic Tennessee setting. The first time we made the journey, the chefs were kind enough to send us specially prepared boxed lunches filled with divine fried chicken, and it was truly love at first bite. In this different but equally delicious recipe, the masa harina used in the coating—typically the main ingredient in Mexican tortillas—makes perfect sense; after all, what could be more Southern than corn? Mimicking the flavors of iced tea in the brine is ingenious; it infuses the chicken with lemony nuances and takes me back to lazy afternoons strolling the grounds, cold glass of sweet tea in hand.

BRINE THE CHICKEN: In a large saucepan, combine the tea, sugar, salt, and lemon quarters and zest. Simmer the mixture over medium-high heat until the salt and sugar dissolve, 5 minutes. Remove from the heat, add 1 quart ice water, allow the brine to cool, then add the chicken to the brine. Refrigerate for 48 hours, then drain the chicken and pat dry.

MAKE THE DREDGE AND DIP: In a large bowl, combine 2 cups of the flour with the masa harina, Old Bay, chili powder, salt, and pepper. In another large bowl, beat the eggs with the buttermilk. Place the remaining 2 cups flour in a third bowl.

DREDGE THE CHICKEN: Roll the chicken in the plain flour, then the buttermilk dip, and then the seasoned dredge. Arrange the legs and thighs in a single layer on a plate or baking sheet. Set aside at room temperature for 30 minutes.

FRY THE CHICKEN: Set a wire rack atop a rimmed baking sheet. Fill a large pot halfway with oil and heat to 300°F. Working in batches, add the chicken and cook until golden and the juices run clear, 22 to 24 minutes. Drain the chicken on the rack and let rest for at least 10 minutes. Serve immediately or at room temperature.

Blackberry Farm's Sweet Tea–Brined Fried Chicken

MICHAEL SOLOMONOV

FEDERAL DONUTS FRIED CHICKEN *and* SAUCE

SERVES 4

FOR THE CHICKEN

1 whole chicken, cut into 8 pieces
Kosher salt for seasoning,
plus 1 tablespoon
Vegetable or canola oil, for frying
2 cups cornstarch
1 cup all-purpose flour

FOR THE SAUCE (MAKES 1⅓ CUPS)

¼ cup chili-garlic sauce,
such as Huy Fong brand
¼ cup soy sauce
¾ cup kecap manis (Malaysian sweet
soy sauce, available at Asian grocers
or online)
3 tablespoons apple cider vinegar

Cake doughnuts and Asian pickles,
for serving

James Beard Award–winning Chef Michael Solomonov's Korean-style fried chicken has pretty much bested the Philly competition since day one. Its thin, shell-like coating and spicy-sweet sauce made with Malaysian kecap manis (sweet soy sauce) are virtually irresistible. At Solomonov's restaurant, Federal Donuts, the chicken sells out early, but thankfully you can make the recipe at home any time you like. In a whimsical take on chicken and waffles, the chicken is served with Federal's house-made cake doughnuts—but feel free to sub in your store-bought variety of choice. If you can't find the kecap manis, mix two parts hoisin sauce to one part soy sauce as a substitute.

SALT THE CHICKEN: The night before cooking the chicken, liberally season the pieces with kosher salt and arrange in a single layer on a rimmed baking sheet. Refrigerate overnight, loosely covered with parchment paper.

MAKE THE SAUCE: In a small bowl, combine the chili-garlic sauce, soy sauce, kecap manis, and vinegar.

FRY THE CHICKEN: Fill a large (at least 8-quart) pot halfway with oil and heat to 300°F. Set a baking rack on top of a rimmed baking sheet and set aside. In a large bowl, whisk together the cornstarch and flour and 1 tablespoon salt, then whisk in 1¾ cups water to make a crepelike batter, adding water by the tablespoonful if the batter feels too thick. Dip the chicken pieces in the batter, shaking off the excess, and fry in batches until the chicken is golden, 12 to 13 minutes.

TWICE-FRY THE CHICKEN: Drain the chicken on the prepared rack and increase the oil temperature to 350°F. Fry the chicken until it is crisp and the color deepens, an additional 5 minutes. Let the chicken cool for 2 to 3 minutes on the rack, then coat the chicken liberally with the sauce (or serve with the sauce on the side). Serve with cake doughnuts and pickles.

The Popeyes Experience

PART I: Sleuthing a Classic

ONE OF MY ALL-TIME FAVORITE versions of fried chicken comes from Popeyes, the New Orleans-inspired chain of fast-food joints founded by Al Copeland in 1972 and named after the Gene Hackman character in *The French Connection*. The combination of crunchy, crenellated crust and juicy meat—all infused with a heady mix of spices—makes for guilty-pleasure eating I never tire of. Popeyes is a cult favorite among regular N'Awlins citizens, and nationwide foodies and chefs alike. Fans have spent considerable time debating the chain's secret ingredients and proprietary techniques (both shrouded in mystery) and posting loving tributes to the company's biscuits and red beans and rice.

From the minute I heard Popeyes had a test kitchen in their corporate headquarters in Atlanta, Georgia, I knew I had to pay them a visit. But how to gain access? I'd been inside some pretty exclusive cooking lairs, but convincing Popeyes to let us in became an intricate negotiation complete with nondisclosure agreements and a reasonable amount of begging. We received our golden ticket from Popeyes chief global branding officer, Dick Lynch. Soon we found ourselves, finally, inside the spacious, industrial-style test kitchen itself in Atlanta. In one corner, white-jacketed workers measured the brix (sugar content) of sauces in development. "Stay away from that area," research and development chef Marshall Scarborough warned us when we tried to take a peek. But then, displaying a surprising amount of transparency, he took us through the paces of making of a

---

OPPOSITE: The finished product: Popeyes Fried Chicken with the signature crispy "nodules"

batch of Popeyes spicy fried chicken as Lynch stood watching nearby.

First, the chicken was seasoned in a proprietary blend of spices poured from unlabeled red packets—though we're pretty sure we spotted cayenne, paprika, onion powder, and garlic powder. The chicken was then transferred to a cylindrical, crank-operated (and possibly vacuum-sealing) chamber and rotated to evenly distribute spices. Franchisees are required to rest the chicken in spices for a minimum of 12 hours, but are given carte blanche to go up to 72 hours. This sliding scale of marinating time might help explain why the chicken at one Popeyes locations is relatively mild, while another's is more deeply spiced. The truly devoted can tell the difference.

Next, the chicken is dipped in a turmeric-hued batter. Then comes the highly ritualistic dredging: flour is tossed around the chicken to coat, but not weigh down, the pieces. The iconic "clapping" we saw all over the South came next: a motion that gently agitates the chicken and banishes excess flour.

Then into the hot oil bath went the coated pieces of bird, emerging crunchy and golden and airy, adorned with fragment-like "nubbins" of crunch that distinguish Popeyes chicken from the competition. Finally, the fried chicken was deposited in tissue-lined boxes for sampling. (Delicious, as always.)

There was just one thing left to do: ask for the recipe. How could we forgive ourselves if we hadn't? After being politely (always politely) rebuffed, we headed out. But in the absence of the recipe for the real thing, we got the perfect substitute: an uncanny imitation from a world-class chef . . .

Inside the mysterious Popeyes test kitchen.

OPPOSITE: Seasoning the chicken in its secret spice blend

LEFT and BELOW: Dipping the chicken into its orangey-yellow batter; fluffing the flour onto the seasoned pieces

PART II: Wylie to the Rescue

WE'D KNOWN FOR A WHILE that chef Wylie Dufresne was a devoted Popeyes fried chicken fan—no other chef we knew had gone so far as to serve it at his wedding. So imagine our delight when Dufresne enthusiastically agreed to create a Popeyes facsimile especially for us!

A pioneer of so-called molecular cooking techniques at his groundbreaking Lower East Side restaurant, WD-50, Dufresne agreed to keep this final recipe simple enough for home cooks—no sous-vide cooking, hydrocolloids, or liquid nitrogen required. We stopped by the immaculate WD-50 kitchen to watch Dufresne demonstrate his iteration of the Popeyes chicken tenders he loves so much. "It's just the most delicious chicken," he said as he sliced skinless, boneless chicken breasts into

2-ounce portions, "and the combo of very crispy skin and very juicy meat is almost impossible to find."

After much sleuthing and hands-on research (courtesy of countless takeout orders from the Popeyes franchise a stone's throw from WD-50), Dufresne decided that rather than aim for either juicy meat or a crispy crust, he wanted to nail both in one fell swoop. He eventually settled on a simple overnight buttermilk marinade, then a breading containing a variety of pulverized, highly flavorful elements: onion soup base and spaghetti-sauce spice mix, both of which pack a wallop of salty and pay homage to the convenience foods Dufresne loves (this is a man, after all, who makes his own American cheese slices). To achieve the craggy, shatteringly dry crust he arrived at a combination of corn and potato starches plus all-purpose flour, and let the chicken rest after breading to allow the coating to adhere.

Then it was time for frying. "I spent two weeks finding a temperature that achieved maximum juiciness and crispiness," he told us as he hovered over his deep-fryer. After five minutes' time bubbling in 300°F in simple canola oil, the tenders emerged golden and perfectly wizened, with crispy stalactites of crust jutting out every which way. They were fall-apart tender, flavorful and crunchy all at the same time—not to mention pretty damned close to the original. "We could have done even better if you'd let us use some of our fancy tricks," said Dufresne with a slight smile. "But I hope we did Popeyes proud."

OPPOSITE and THIS PAGE: Wylie and his process for his Popeyes facsimile recipe

POPEYES-STYLE CHICKEN TENDERS
and Biscuits

SERVES 4 TO 6

FOR THE BRINE

1½	pounds skinless, boneless chicken breasts, cut into 12 2-ounce chicken tenders
4	cups buttermilk
1	teaspoon Louisiana-style hot sauce, such as Crystal (or more to taste)

FOR THE BREADING

3	cups (13.5 ounces) self-rising flour
½	cup (2 ¼ ounces) cornstarch
½	cup (2 ¼ ounces) potato starch
2	tablespoons (1 ounce) sea salt, plus more for seasoning
4	tablespoons (1 ounce) paprika
1	teaspoon (.176 ounce) baking soda
2	tablespoons (1 ounce) onion soup base, ground in spice grinder until fine
7	teaspoons (1 ounce) Italian Herb Spaghetti Sauce Seasoning Mix (see Note), finely ground

Canola oil for frying

A tamis is a sifting tool, typically made of a very fine piece of mesh stretched over a round frame.

This recipe is Dufresne's edible paean to the Popeyes chicken tenders he loves, as well as a tasty facsimile of Popeyes biscuits. "You can't have one without the other," he reasoned. Using vegetable shortening and powdered milk achieves a rich, flaky, light-as-air biscuit worthy of its snack-box counterpart. To honor Dufresne's mad scientist method, we've kept his original metric measurements in place, but you can convert as you like.

Dufresne found the flavor combination in McCormick's Italian Herb Spaghetti Sauce Seasoning Mix (available in most grocery stores and online) to be the most pleasing for its blend of traditional chicken breading spices. If you can't find it, grind 2 teaspoons each sugar, salt, and dehydrated onions with 1 teaspoon each dried basil and oregano and ½ teaspoon each chile flakes, black pepper, and garlic powder.

BRINE THE CHICKEN: In a large, nonreactive bowl or Ziploc bag combine the chicken, buttermilk, and hot sauce; cover and refrigerate overnight.

BREAD THE CHICKEN: Sift all breading ingredients 3 times through a flour tamis (see Note) or very fine mesh strainer into a large bowl, discarding any lumps. Working in batches, remove 4 or 5 tenders at a time from the buttermilk marinade and toss in the breading, coating well. Transfer to a baking sheet and let rest until the breading adheres, 15 to 20 minutes.

FRY THE CHICKEN: While the chicken rests, add 2 inches of oil to a large (at least 6-quart) pot and heat to 300°F. Working in batches, fry 4 to 5 tenders at a time until brown and crisp, 5 minutes per batch. Remove to a paper towel to drain. Once all the chicken is fried, season lightly with salt and serve with the biscuits.

POPEYES BUTTERMILK BISCUITS
MAKES 12 BISCUITS (WITH ENOUGH FLOUR MIX FOR A SECOND BATCH)

FOR THE BISCUIT BASE

- 4 cups (17.6 ounces) all-purpose flour
- ½ cup (2.11 ounces) nonfat powdered milk
- 4 teaspoons (.7 ounces) baking powder
- 1 teaspoon (.176 ounces) salt
- 1 packed cup (5.7 ounces) vegetable shortening

FOR THE BISCUIT MIXTURE

- 3 tablespoons (1.67 ounces) sour cream
- 3 tablespoons (1.75 ounces) buttermilk
  Scant ½ cup club soda (3.527 ounces)
  Melted butter for brushing the biscuits

MAKE THE BISCUIT BASE: Preheat oven to 375°F. In a large bowl sift the flour, milk powder, baking powder, and salt. Using two knives or a pastry blender, cut in the shortening until small, pea-sized pieces remain. (The biscuit base can be refrigerated and stored for up to 1 month.)

MAKE THE BISCUITS: In a large bowl mix half the Biscuit Base (about 2¾ cups) with the sour cream, then add the buttermilk and club soda and gently stir until just incorporated. On a well-floured work surface, gently roll out the dough to ¾-inch thickness and generously flour the top. Using a three-inch biscuit cutter, cut out the biscuits and arrange on a parchment-lined baking sheet.

BAKE THE BISCUITS: Brush the biscuits liberally with melted butter and bake until lightly golden, 20 to 22 minutes. Serve immediately.

Wylie Dufresne's Popeyes Style Chicken Tenders

"MY ROOTS ARE THE INDIAN

South; my home is the American South," says Asha Gomez, chef-owner of Atlanta's Cardamom Hill. Growing up on the beach in Kerala, a region of India whose cuisine reflects its Christian-Portuguese influence, Gomez was exposed to a host of ingredients—sorghum, pork, coconut, and rice among them— that she was surprised to find in abundance when she moved to Georgia at age 16. Her fragrant, crunchy fried chicken, marinated overnight in an emerald-green purée of buttermilk, herbs, and spices before breading, is a revelation. The accompanying rice-studded Lowcountry waffles, topped with spice-infused maple syrup and flash-fried curry leaves, brilliantly connect the dots between her culinary past and present.

ASHA GOMEZ

KERALAN FRIED CHICKEN,
Lowcountry Cardamom Waffles, and Spicy Maple Syrup

SERVES 8

FOR THE SPICY MAPLE SYRUP

- 2 teaspoons whole cumin seeds, coarsely ground
- 2 teaspoons whole coriander seeds, coarsely ground
- 1 teaspoon crushed red pepper flakes
- 2 cups maple syrup

FOR THE CHICKEN

- 2 cups buttermilk
- 10 garlic cloves
- 1 2-inch piece fresh ginger, peeled
- 6 whole serrano (or 3 large jalapeño) peppers, seeded if desired
  Bunch of fresh cilantro
  Bunch of fresh mint
- 2 tablespoons kosher salt
- 8 boneless, skin-on chicken thighs (about 3 pounds)
  Vegetable oil, for frying
- 4 cups all-purpose flour
- 2 tablespoons coconut oil, melted
- 2 stems fresh curry leaves

MAKE THE SYRUP: Toast the cumin, coriander, and red pepper flakes in a dry, hot medium skillet until fragrant, 1 to 2 minutes. Whisk the toasted spices into the maple syrup and let the syrup infuse at room temperature for 24 hours.

MARINATE THE CHICKEN: In a blender, purée the buttermilk, garlic, ginger, peppers, cilantro, mint, and salt until smooth. Place the chicken in a large glass dish or bowl, pour the buttermilk purée over the chicken, toss to coat, and refrigerate for 24 hours.

FRY THE CHICKEN: Fill a large (12-inch) cast-iron skillet with ⅓ inch oil and gently heat to 350°F. Set a wire rack on top of a rimmed baking sheet and set aside. While the oil is heating, remove the chicken from the buttermilk purée, gently shake off excess, and dredge each piece in flour. Place the chicken in the skillet, skin side down; the oil should come halfway up the pan. Cook the chicken until it turns golden brown, 4 minutes per side. Drain the chicken on the rack and drizzle with the melted coconut oil. While the chicken is draining, crisp the curry leaves by frying in the oil until crisp, 10 to 15 seconds.

TO SERVE: Serve the chicken on top of the waffles and drizzle with the spiced syrup. Garnish with the fried curry leaves.

OPPOSITE: Asha Gomez with her emerald-green fried chicken

CARDAMOM WAFFLES

MAKES 8 WAFFLES

1½ cups all-purpose flour
½ cup rice flour
¼ cup unsweetened malt powder
(available online)
2 tablespoons (packed) light brown sugar
2 teaspoons baking powder
2 teaspoons baking soda
1 teaspoon ground cardamom
1 teaspoon salt
2 large eggs
2½ cups buttermilk
6 tablespoons unsalted butter, melted and cooled,
plus more for greasing the waffle iron
½ cup cooked basmati or white rice

In a large bowl, whisk together the flour, rice flour, malt powder, sugar, baking powder, baking soda, cardamom, and salt. In a separate bowl, whisk together the eggs, then add the buttermilk and melted butter and whisk again.

Slowly whisk the wet mixture into the dry ingredients, then add the cooked rice, whisking just until combined. Cover and let the batter rest for about 1 hour at room temperature.

Heat a waffle iron and brush with melted butter. For each waffle, ladle ½ cup batter into the waffle iron and cook until crisp and golden, 4 to 5 minutes.

IF CHARLES GABRIEL (see page 52) represents a classic taste of Harlem, chef Marcus Samuelsson is one of its newest, boldest faces. His Lenox Avenue restaurant, Red Rooster, has been a magnet for locals and far beyond since its opening in 2010, with dishes that pay homage to the immediate surroundings while nodding to Samuelsson's Ethiopian and Swedish heritage. Over the years Samuelsson has developed various fried chicken recipes, but the one he shared with us is decidedly different. "I didn't want to compete with the neighborhood classics," he said. Instead, he brines boneless thighs in coffee and lemon to tenderize. Then, inspired by the classic Belgian method for double-cooked, extra-crispy French fries, he braises the chicken in a potent brew of buttermilk, lime, chile, and red curry paste at a low temperature before breading in Panko bread crumbs and a spice blend that includes berbere, Ethiopia's signature spice blend. A second frying results in ultra-crisp chicken, enhanced by the one-two punch of coconut collard greens and a complex gravy. This recipe may have many components, but the finished product—as nuanced as the chef who created it—is well worth the effort.

MARCUS SAMUELSSON

COCONUT FRIED CHICKEN
with Collards and Gravy

SERVES 6

FOR THE BRINE

½ cup brewed coffee
3 tablespoons freshly squeezed
   lemon juice
1 tablespoon kosher salt
12 boneless, skinless chicken thighs
   (2½ to 3 pounds)
   Salt and freshly ground black
   pepper to taste.

FOR THE PICKLING JUICE (MAKES ½ CUP)

2 tablespoons white wine
¼ cup sugar
1 bay leaf
1 allspice berry

FOR THE GRAVY

4 slices bacon, chopped
2 garlic cloves, minced
2 shallots, minced
2 tablespoons pickling juice
   (see above)
½ cup red wine
2 cups beef or chicken stock
2 tablespoons maple syrup
½ cup heavy cream
1 teaspoon whole-grain Dijon
   mustard
1 sprig fresh tarragon, chopped
2 teaspoons chopped dill pickles
2 teaspoons bourbon
2 tablespoons unsalted butter

BRINE THE CHICKEN: Combine 1 cup water with the coffee, lemon juice, and salt in a nonreactive container. Add the chicken, then cover and brine in the refrigerator for 2 hours. Drain and pat the chicken dry with paper towels and season with salt and pepper to taste. Discard the brine.

MAKE THE PICKLING JUICE: In a very small saucepan bring all the ingredients to a boil with ⅓ cup water. Reduce the heat and simmer until the sugar is dissolved, about 1 minute. Remove the saucepan from the heat and cool completely. (The pickling juice can be refrigerated in a sealed container for up to 1 month.)

MAKE THE GRAVY: In a 3- or 4-quart saucepan, sauté the bacon over medium-high heat until the fat begins to render, 1 to 2 minutes. Add the garlic and shallots and cook until golden brown and crispy, 8 minutes. Add 2 tablespoons of the pickling juice, the wine, stock, and maple syrup to the pan. Cook, stirring occasionally, until reduced by half, about 15 minutes. Reduce the heat to medium-low, add the cream, mustard, and tarragon and continue cooking until slightly thickened, 4 to 5 minutes. Stir in the pickles, bourbon, and butter and simmer until the liquid becomes a thick sauce, 4 to 5 minutes. Remove from heat and keep warm.

MAKE THE COLLARDS: In a large, high-sided skillet, cook the bacon until crisp. Drain the bacon on paper towels, then crumble into small pieces. In a small saucepan, bring the coconut milk and soy sauce to a boil. Remove from the heat and stir in the mustard and crumbled bacon. Using the same skillet used for the bacon, heat the olive oil and butter over low heat. Add the garlic and slowly toast until pale golden brown, about 10 minutes. (Be careful not to let it burn). Lift the garlic out of the oil with a slotted spoon

- 6 slices bacon
- ½ cup coconut milk
- ¼ cup reduced-sodium soy sauce
- 1 tablespoon whole-grain Dijon mustard
- 3 tablespoons olive oil
- 1 tablespoon unsalted butter
- 4 garlic cloves, peeled and halved
- 1 pound collard greens, ribs removed, leaves thinly shredded (6 cups)
- 1 pound bok choy, very thinly sliced (6 cups)

FOR SAUTÉING THE CHICKEN

- 3 tablespoons peanut oil
- 2 garlic cloves, chopped
- 1 to 2 Scotch bonnet chiles, seeded (optional) and chopped
- 2 tablespoons red curry paste
- ½ cup coconut milk
- ½ cup buttermilk
- ⅓ cup brewed coffee
- ¼ cup freshly squeezed lime juice

FOR THE CHICKEN SHAKE (MAKES 1 CUP)

- ½ tablespoon garlic powder
- 2 tablespoons celery salt
- 2 tablespoons ground cumin
- ¼ cup berbere spice
- ¼ cup smoked hot paprika
- ½ tablespoon kosher salt
- 2 tablespoons ground white pepper
- ½ teaspoon ground coffee

FOR BREADING AND FRYING

- 4 cups peanut oil
- 2 cups panko bread crumbs
- 4 tablespoons cornstarch
- 4 egg whites

and set aside; remove and discard all but 3 tablespoons fat from the skillet. Add the collards and cook, stirring frequently, until the greens start to wilt, about 2 minutes. Stir in the coconut milk mixture and cook until the greens are tender and the sauce has thickened, 13 to 15 minutes. Add the bok choy and cook, stirring, until wilted but still tender-crisp, 3 to 4 minutes. Stir in the reserved garlic; remove from heat and cover to keep warm.

SAUTÉ THE CHICKEN: Heat the peanut oil in a 12-inch sauté pan over medium-high heat. Once again season the chicken with salt and pepper. Working in batches, add the chicken and brown on both sides, 2 minutes per side. Remove the chicken from the pan and set aside. Into the same pan, add the garlic, chiles, and curry paste and sauté over medium heat until golden and fragrant, about 3 minutes. Add the coconut milk, buttermilk, coffee, lime juice, and 1 cup of water and return the chicken to the pan. Bring to a simmer and cook uncovered until the chicken is cooked through, about 10 to 12 minutes. Remove from the heat and set aside to cool.

MAKE THE CHICKEN SHAKE: In a small bowl whisk all ingredients until incorporated. (The Chicken Shake can be stored in an airtight container for up to 6 months.)

BREAD THE CHICKEN: Fill a large (at least 12-inch) cast-iron skillet with 1½ inches oil and heat to 350° F. While the oil is heating, in a shallow bowl combine the panko, cornstarch, and 1 tablespoon of the Chicken Shake. In another shallow, wide bowl, whisk the egg whites together. Dip the chicken in the egg white, then roll in the panko-cornstarch mix, coating well.

FRY THE CHICKEN: Working in 2 batches, carefully add the chicken pieces to the oil and fry until golden brown, 2 to 3 minutes per side. Drain on paper towels and season with additional salt to taste.

Serve the chicken with collards and gravy.

HONEY'S KETTLE HOME-STYLE SMASHED GARLIC FRIED CHICKEN

SERVES 4

FOR DRY-MARINATING THE CHICKEN

- 2 tablespoons onion powder
- 2 tablespoons ground cumin
- 2 tablespoons kosher salt
- 2 tablespoons garlic powder
- 1 tablespoon ground allspice
- 1½ teaspoons cayenne pepper
- 1 whole chicken, cut into 13 pieces (breasts and thighs halved, back reserved for frying)

FOR THE COATING MIX

- 2 cups cake flour
- 1 cup plus 2 tablespoons yellow cornmeal
- ½ cup plain bread crumbs
- 1 tablespoon plus 1 teaspoon kosher salt
- ¼ cup onion powder
- ¼ cup garlic powder
- ¼ cup sesame seeds
- 2 tablespoons ground marjoram
- 1 garlic clove, smashed
- 1 tablespoon cayenne pepper
- 1 tablespoon coriander seeds
- 1 tablespoon ground sage
- 1 tablespoon ground allspice
- 1 teaspoon freshly ground black pepper

FOR FRYING

- Canola oil
- 1 cup whole milk
- 5 to 7 garlic cloves, peeled and smashed (or more, if desired)

We first contacted Honey's Kettle in Culver City, California, with the hope of convincing chef/owner Vincent Williams to give up his formula for lacy, batter-dipped chicken. Instead, he concocted one of the most original recipes we've tried to date. The chicken is marinated in a thick paste of spices (the longer it sits in the fridge, the better), battered in a seasoned slurry, then passed through heavily seasoned flour before skillet-frying. With its toasty whole seeds and crackerlike crust, this dish reminds us that fried chicken is open to constant reinvention.

MARINATE THE CHICKEN: In a large bowl, blend the onion powder, cumin, salt, garlic powder, allspice, and cayenne pepper together with a fork. Rinse the chicken thoroughly with cold water, but do not pat dry. Add the chicken to the bowl and toss to coat thoroughly with the seasoning. Cover and refrigerate for at least 2 hours or overnight.

MAKE THE COATING MIX: Blend all ingredients in a large bowl.

DREDGE THE CHICKEN: Pour 2 inches oil into a 12- or 14-inch cast-iron skillet and gently heat to 375°F. Set a wire rack over a rimmed baking sheet and set aside. Pour the milk into a large bowl. Add 1 cup of the coating mix to the milk and whisk to create a slurry with the consistency of pancake batter. Dip the chicken in the slurry, then in the remaining coating mix. (For extra-crunchy results, repeat the process to create an extra-thick crust.)

FRY THE CHICKEN: Working in batches, add the chicken to the skillet; oil temperature will drop to 350°F. Fry at 350°F until the underside is deep golden brown, 8 to 9 minutes. Flip the chicken, add the garlic cloves, and fry until the garlic and chicken are golden brown, 7 to 8 minutes. Drain the chicken and garlic on the rack for 7 minutes and serve immediately.

MARK ROMANO

HIGHLAND KITCHEN'S FRIED (CHICKEN)
and Frozen (Cocktail)

CHICKEN SERVES 4; COCKTAIL SERVES 1

FOR THE BRINE

- ½ cup kosher salt
- 1 whole chicken, cut into 10 pieces
- 4 cups buttermilk

FOR THE DREDGE

- 4 cups all-purpose flour
- 1¾ cups cornstarch
- 1 cup Maseca (instant Mexican corn flour) or masa harina
- 2 tablespoons kosher salt
- 1 tablespoon paprika
- 1 tablespoon onion powder
- 1 tablespoon garlic powder
- 1 tablespoon ground coriander
- 1 tablespoon celery salt
- 1½ teaspoons freshly ground black pepper

  Vegetable oil, for frying

With a two-day brining process and a super-crunchy coating coaxed into crispness in part by the addition of Maseca—a finely milled variation on masa harina found at Mexican markets—it's no wonder Chef Mark Romano preps for a large crowd at Boston's Highland Kitchen. Like many of his nightly specials, this one is served with a cocktail, in this case a frozen mango concoction that delivers an extra kick courtesy of Scotch bonnet peppers.

BRINE THE CHICKEN: In a large bowl, whisk the salt with 8 cups cold water. Add the chicken, cover, and refrigerate overnight or up to 24 hours. Drain and discard the brine, pour the buttermilk over the chicken, cover, and refrigerate overnight or up to 24 hours.

MAKE THE DREDGE: In a large bowl, whisk together the flour, cornstarch, Maseca, salt, paprika, onion powder, garlic powder, coriander, celery salt, and pepper.

FRY THE CHICKEN: Fill a large pot halfway with oil and heat to 350°F. Set a wire rack on top of a rimmed baking sheet and set aside. Remove the chicken from the buttermilk (don't rinse it!) and dredge the chicken in the flour mixture. Working in batches, fry the chicken until the internal temperature of the white pieces reaches 160°F, and the dark pieces reach 165°F, on a deep-fry thermometer (13 to 14 minutes for breasts and 16 to 17 minutes for thighs). Rest the chicken on the rack while you make the cocktail. Serve the chicken with the cocktail and your favorite biscuits.

FROZEN COCKTAIL

Frozen mango purée can be found at many Latin markets or gourmet markets. The pepper-infused syrup makes enough for 3 cocktails.

½ cup plus 2 tablespoons lime juice
½ cup sugar
½ whole Scotch bonnet pepper
1 2-inch piece fresh ginger, peeled and sliced
3 crushed cardamom pods
5 allspice berries
1½ ounces anejo rum
¼ cup mango purée
　 Dash of angostura bitters

In a small saucepan, combine ½ cup of the lime juice with the sugar, pepper, ginger, cardamom, and allspice and bring to a boil. Reduce the heat and simmer until the juice is no longer cloudy, about 5 minutes. Strain and discard the solids. In a blender, combine 3 tablespoons of the lime syrup (reserve remaining syrup for additional cocktails) with the remaining 2 tablespoons lime juice, the rum, the mango purée, and 2 cups ice. Blend until smooth and finish with a dash of angostura bitters.

MICHAEL ROMANO

GRAHAM CRACKER–CRUSTED CHICKEN

SERVES 4

1 whole chicken (3 to 3 ½ pounds), cut into 10 pieces
2 cups buttermilk
1 cup all-purpose flour
1 cup panko bread crumbs
1 cup graham cracker crumbs
2 tablespoons paprika
2 tablespoons kosher salt
1 tablespoon garlic powder
¾ teaspoon cayenne pepper
Vegetable oil, for frying

Michael Romano's love of fried chicken originates with his mother's crumb-dipped cutlets. These days, his work for the Union Square Hospitality Group often takes him to Japan, and he satisfies his fried chicken craving with panko-crusted, deep-fried pork tonkatsu. *This recipe, which first appeared during "family meal" at Romano's Union Square Café, is a combination of both influences: the graham crackers lend subtle, toasty sweetness, and the panko contributes an unmatchable crunch.*

DREDGE THE CHICKEN: Place the chicken pieces in a large bowl, add the buttermilk, and let soak for 30 minutes at room temperature, turning occasionally. In a medium bowl, whisk together the flour, panko, graham cracker crumbs, paprika, salt, garlic powder, and cayenne pepper. Drain the chicken pieces and dredge in the seasoned flour, shaking off the excess.

FRY THE CHICKEN: In a large, deep cast-iron skillet, heat 2 inches oil over medium-high heat until it reaches 325°F on a deep-fry thermometer. Using tongs and working in batches, carefully add the chicken and fry until the interior temperature of a thigh reaches 165°F on an instant-read thermometer, 6 minutes per side for wings and legs and 8 minutes per side for breasts and thighs. Drain on paper towels and serve hot.

> *Graham crackers tend to brown faster than traditional flour or even panko, so keep a close eye on each piece, removing it as soon as you think it's done.*

MARIO CARBONE AND RICH TORRISI

PARM'S FRIED CHICKEN CACCIATORE

SERVES 4

FOR THE CHICKEN MARINADE

½ cup dried black trumpet, porcini, or other dried mushrooms

1 cup Greek yogurt

1 teaspoon smoked paprika

1 teaspoon tomato paste

½ teaspoon garlic powder

½ teaspoon onion powder

1 teaspoon kosher salt

¼ teaspoon dried rosemary

1 whole chicken, cut into 8 pieces

FOR THE AGRODOLCE SAUCE

1 cup red wine vinegar

1 cup sugar

The Monday-night special continues be a catalyst for fried chicken creativity. That's certainly the case at New York City's Parm restaurant, where chefs Rich Torrisi and Mario Carbone serve dressed-down Italian favorites reinterpreted with power-chef savvy and cutting-edge techniques. Here, they set out to put their own spin on chicken cacciatore. The traditional recipe, which translates into "hunter's chicken," invariably includes skillet-browned chicken parts simmered in a mushroom- and tomato-based sauce. They swap in a yogurt-cloaked, Southern-fried bird—a technique Mario learned from Chef Laurent Tourondel—then replace the traditional sliced fungi with an easy-to-make mushroom powder that feels modern and comforting at the same time.

MARINATE THE CHICKEN: Pick through the mushrooms to remove any stones or woody pieces, then place them in a coffee or spice grinder and grind to a fine powder. In a large bowl, whisk 1 teaspoon of the mushroom powder with the yogurt, smoked paprika, tomato paste, garlic powder, onion powder, salt, and rosemary until everything is well blended. Add the chicken pieces and turn to coat in the yogurt mixture. Arrange the chicken in a single layer on a parchment-lined baking sheet. Refrigerate, uncovered, for 24 hours.

MAKE THE AGRODOLCE SAUCE: In a small saucepan, stir together the vinegar and sugar; bring the liquid to a boil, then reduce the heat to medium and cook until the liquid has reduced to 1 cup, 15 to 17 minutes. Remove from the heat, let the sauce cool completely, and pour it into an empty plastic squeeze bottle or honey bear bottle.

(continued)

¼ cup olive oil
2 garlic cloves, minced
1 sprig fresh rosemary, leaves only
½ teaspoon chile flakes
3 to 4 bacon slices, finely diced
½ cup finely diced onion
¼ cup finely diced celery
¼ cup finely diced carrot
1 teaspoon kosher salt,
   plus more to taste
¼ teaspoon freshly ground black
   pepper, plus more to taste
¼ cup tomato paste
¼ cup dry white wine
1 cup canned crushed tomatoes
½ cup chicken stock

FOR FRYING

   Vegetable oil
2 cups all-purpose flour
1 tablespoon coarsely ground
   black pepper

MAKE THE CACCIATORE SAUCE: Heat the olive oil in a large saucepan over medium heat. Add the garlic, rosemary, and chile flakes and cook until fragrant, 1 to 2 minutes. Add the bacon and onion and cook, stirring constantly, until the onion begins to soften, about 5 minutes. Add the celery, carrot, salt, and pepper and cook, stirring, until the vegetables soften, 6 to 7 minutes. Add the tomato paste and an additional tablespoon of the mushroom powder and cook, stirring, until the vegetable mixture turns brick-red in color, about 2 minutes. Add the wine and cook until the liquid has reduced by half, 2 minutes. Add the tomatoes and stock and cook, stirring, until incorporated and thickened, about 5 minutes; if the sauce is too thick, add water by the tablespoonful to thin out the sauce to the desired consistency. Season with additional salt and pepper.

FRY THE CHICKEN: Set a rack over a baking sheet and set aside. Prepare a deep-fryer or fill a large pot halfway with oil and heat to 365°F. Preheat the oven to 350°F. In a bowl, combine the flour and pepper. Dredge the chicken in the flour mixture. Working in batches, fry the chicken until the internal temperature reaches between 155°F and 160°F, moving chicken around occasionally to prevent sticking, about 9 minutes per piece. Transfer the chicken to the rack and bake until it deepens slightly in color and achieves an internal temperature of 165°F, 7 to 8 minutes. Season with salt and pepper to taste.

TO SERVE: Transfer the finished chicken to a platter and top with the cacciatore sauce. Serve with the agrodolce sauce on the side.

LOUISIANA BATTERED FRIED CHICKEN

SERVES 4

FOR THE CHICKEN MARINADE

- 1 whole chicken, cut into 8 pieces
- 1 tablespoon kosher salt
- 1 tablespoon Cajun seasoning
- 2 teaspoons freshly ground black pepper
- 1½ teaspoons cayenne pepper
- 1½ teaspoons garlic powder
- 1 teaspoon paprika

FOR THE FLOUR DUST DREDGE

- 3 cups all-purpose flour
- 2 tablespoons kosher salt
- 1 tablespoon freshly ground black pepper

FOR THE HOT TUB DIP

- 3 cups all-purpose flour
- 2½ tablespoons cornstarch
- 3 large egg yolks
- 1 tablespoon Louisiana hot sauce
- 2 teaspoons freshly ground black pepper
- 1½ cups cold beer (*not* extra-dark)
- 1½ tablespoons lemon juice

  Peanut oil, for frying

One of country music's biggest stars, Zac Brown is a chart-topper whose hits include the anthem "Chicken Fried" and who is known for his close relationship with his devoted audience. Brown's road chef, Rusty Hamlin, prepares a family-style "eat-and-greet" meal for two hundred die-hard fans before every show. Working out of a 53-foot state-of-the-art kitchen on wheels affectionately nicknamed "Cookie," Hamlin procures and prepares local produce alongside his own signature dishes. Seeing as one of Brown's biggest hits is named after our favorite dish, we asked Chef Rusty if he had a fried chicken recipe up his sleeve. He did one better, developing this spicy, beer-battered version—inspired by his childhood in Baton Rouge and a love of all things Louisiana—just for us.

MARINATE THE CHICKEN: In a Ziploc bag, combine the chicken and all the marinade ingredients, then seal and shake to distribute the spices over the meat. Press out all the air in the bag and seal tightly. Refrigerate the chicken overnight or up to 24 hours.

PREPARE THE FLOUR DUST AND HOT TUB DIP: Set 2 wire racks over rimmed baking sheets. In one large mixing bowl, combine the flour, salt, and pepper to make the flour dust. In another large mixing bowl, whisk together all the Hot Tub Dip ingredients with 1½ cups cold water until all lumps disappear, about 1 minute.

DREDGE THE CHICKEN: Fill a 6- or 8-quart cast-iron Dutch oven halfway with oil and heat to 350°F. Working one piece at a time, dredge the chicken pieces in the dip, shaking off the excess. Dredge the pieces in the flour dust, coating well. Place the prepared pieces on a reserved wire rack until ready to fry.

FRY THE CHICKEN: Working in batches, gently place the chicken in the oil, regulating the temperature at around 325°F, and fry until the pieces are golden brown and the internal temperature reaches 165°F, 14 to 15 minutes. Drain the chicken on the other wire rack; let rest for 10 minutes and serve warm.

SENEGALESE FRIED CHICKEN

SERVES 4

FOR THE SEASONING

- 1 cup peanut flour
- 2 teaspoons sea salt
- 1 teaspoon ground ginger
- 1 teaspoon onion powder
- 1 teaspoon garlic powder
- 1 teaspoon cayenne pepper
- ½ teaspoon freshly ground black pepper
- 1 whole chicken, cut into 8 pieces

FOR FRYING

- Peanut oil
- 2 cups all-purpose flour

- Fried plantains and sautéed greens, for serving

Harlem is home to a vibrant West African immigrant community, and on West 116th Street, also known as Little Senegal, you can have your hair braided in the traditional style, outfit yourself in gorgeous African robes, or eat French-African food to the percussive, melodic beats of Baaba Maal, Youssou N'Dour, or African hip-hop. This spicy, nutty recipe comes to us courtesy of chef and caterer Pierre Thiam, who in turn adapted it from nomadic Hausa tribesmen in his native Senegal. Thiam marinates his chicken parts in a variety of spices along with finely milled peanut flour, which gives the crust a nutty, feathery crunch. The peanut flour can be found in African markets or some health food stores. You can also process unsalted, unroasted peanuts in the food processor until very fine; just make sure to pulse toward the end to avoid making peanut butter.

MAKE THE SEASONING: In a large bowl, combine the peanut flour, salt, ground ginger, onion powder, garlic powder, cayenne pepper, and black pepper. Add the chicken pieces to the bowl, coat in the peanut mixture, cover, and refrigerate overnight.

FRY THE CHICKEN: Fill a deep-fryer or a large pot halfway with oil and heat to 350°F. Set a rack over a rimmed baking sheet and set aside. Place the all-purpose flour in a large bowl and dredge the chilled, peanut-coated chicken in the flour. Working in batches, fry the chicken until golden, 13 to 14 minutes. Transfer to the rack, cool slightly, and serve with fried plantains and sautéed greens.

IN THE KITCHEN AT ATLANTA'S
*acclaimed Watershed, Steven
Satterfield fried thousands of
chickens before opening his own
restaurant, Miller Union, in 2009.
One night a couple of years back,
pressed into service to cook a
charity dinner at a patron's home,
Satterfield found himself without
the buttermilk he typically uses
to marinate his birds. Concerted
refrigerator-foraging yielded
Greek yogurt, which tenderized
the chicken and encouraged an
extra-thick, crunchy coating to
boot. The combination of simply
charred vegetables (to avoid
sliminess, make sure to get the
freshest okra you can find) and
sweet, tangy glaze is signature
Satterfield: deceptively simple
accompaniments that wear their
Southern identity with ease but
could be comfortable on a plate in
any state.*

STEVEN SATTERFIELD

YOGURT-MARINATED CHICKEN THIGHS,
Charred Vegetables, and Honey-Vinegar Glaze

SERVES 8

FOR THE MARINADE

- 2 cups whole-milk Greek yogurt
- ¼ cup Sriracha sauce
- 1 teaspoon kosher salt
- 8 boneless, skin-on chicken thighs, pounded ¼ inch thick (ask your butcher to do this)

FOR THE DREDGE

- 2 cups rice flour
- 2 cups bleached white cake flour, or regular cake flour
- 1 cup cornstarch
- 1 teaspoon fine sea salt
- 1 teaspoon freshly ground black pepper

  Canola or peanut oil, for frying

FOR THE GLAZE

- 1 cup sherry vinegar
- 1 cup honey
- 1 medium jalapeño or serrano pepper, seeded and finely minced

FOR THE VEGETABLES

- 3 cups very fresh okra (about 1 pound), trimmed
- 1 large yellow onion, peeled, trimmed, and cut into wedges
- 2 medium Roma or hothouse tomatoes, quartered
- 2 tablespoons olive oil
  Kosher salt and freshly ground black pepper, to taste

MARINATE THE CHICKEN: Combine the yogurt, Sriracha sauce, and salt in a baking dish. Add the chicken to the dish and toss to coat it with the marinade. Cover and refrigerate for at least 2 to and up to 6 hours.

DREDGE THE CHICKEN: In a baking dish, combine the rice flour, cake flour, cornstarch, salt, and pepper. Remove the chicken from the yogurt mixture, shaking off the excess but not scraping off the residual yogurt. Dredge in the flour mixture, packing on the mixture until completely coated.

FRY THE CHICKEN: Prepare a deep fryer or fill a large (at least 6-quart) pot halfway with oil and heat to 325°F. Fry the chicken until crisp and browned, about 10 minutes. Remove the chicken from the heat and drain on paper towels or keep warm in a low oven.

MAKE THE GLAZE: In a medium saucepan, bring the vinegar, honey, and jalapeño to a boil. Reduce the heat and cook, simmering, until the glaze has thickened enough to coat a spoon, about 10 minutes (the glaze will thicken as it cools).

MAKE THE VEGETABLES: Heat a cast-iron skillet over high heat. Add the okra, onion, and tomatoes in batches and cook until charred, 4 to 5 minutes total. Toss gently in the olive oil and season with salt and pepper.

TO SERVE: Serve the chicken with the vegetables and drizzle the glaze on top.

CHICKEN BONNE FEMME

SERVES 4

1 whole chicken, cut into 8 pieces
Garlic powder to taste
Kosher salt and freshly ground black pepper to taste
Vegetable oil, for frying
1 large Idaho potato (about 1 pound), or 2 small
Red cabbage leaves, for garnish
1½ cups chopped fresh parsley
⅓ cup chopped fresh garlic

Cooks can be deliberately evasive about their recipes. After all, who wants to give up trade secrets unless they need to? So when we pressed Brenda Gooden for details about the garlicky, potato-topped chicken bonne femme ("good woman's chicken") she's been preparing at Tujague's restaurant in New Orleans's French Quarter for the past forty-four years, we weren't entirely surprised when she was short on specifics. The second-oldest restaurant in New Orleans, Tujague's is a standard-bearer of classic Creole cuisine; sitting down to its traditional table d'hôte (fixed) dinner feels like a NOLA history lesson condensed into one meal. Originally patronized by day laborers in the 1850s, the restaurant has played host to every notable politician and musician in town. Though it has changed hands several times—most recently in 1982—some things remain constant, like that chicken bonne femme. In this iteration, the chicken is slaked with salt, pepper, and garlic powder before pan-frying, batterless, in a skillet. Crispy fresh fried silver dollar potatoes and a bracing layer of chopped parsley and garlic complete the picture. Now we know why Brenda was so mysterious about that recipe: its secret is in its simplicity. A "good woman," indeed.

SEASON THE CHICKEN: Preheat the oven to 250°F. Rinse and thoroughly pat dry the chicken and season liberally all over with garlic powder, salt, and pepper.

FRY THE CHICKEN: Heat ½ inch oil in a large skillet over medium-high heat. Working in batches, place the chicken, skin side down, in the skillet and cook, being careful not to move it, until the skin is crispy, 8 to 10 minutes. Flip the chicken and cook until the internal temperature is 165°F, an additional 8 to 10 minutes. Transfer the pieces to a wire rack set over a rimmed baking sheet, cover with foil, and keep warm in the oven.

(continued)

FRY THE POTATOES: Add more oil so it reaches halfway up the sides of the skillet, and heat until very hot but not smoking. While the oil is heating, slice the potatoes to ⅛-inch thickness using a mandoline or sharp knife (it is okay if some are slightly thicker than others). Fry the potato slices in batches until they are crisp and golden, 2 to 3 minutes. Drain on paper towels and season liberally with salt.

TO SERVE: Arrange the cabbage leaves on a serving platter and top with the chicken pieces. Top with the potatoes, then with the parsley and garlic. Season with more salt and pepper to taste.

ABOVE: One of Tujague's longtime cooks, Brenda Gooden
OPPOSITE: Tujague's in the French Quarter by night

FRIED CHICKEN *and* CAULIFLOWER MASH

SERVES 8

FOR THE BRINE

- 1 cup sugar
- 1 cup kosher salt
- 1 scant cup paprika
- 1 scant cup cayenne pepper
- 2 tablespoons freshly ground black pepper
- 2 whole chickens, each cut into 8 pieces

FOR THE SMOKY SPICY PEPPER MIX

- ¼ cup paprika
- 2 tablespoons kosher salt
- 2 tablespoons chili powder

FOR THE STICKY HOT SAUCE

- 2 tablespoons canola oil
- 10 fresh red chiles (about 8 ounces), preferably Tabasco or Fresno, halved lengthwise and seeded (optional)
- 2 garlic cloves, peeled and smashed
- 2 cups red wine vinegar
- 1 tablespoon cornstarch dissolved in 1 tablespoon water
- ¼ cup honey
- ½ teaspoon sea salt

After bringing a breath of fresh air to the Miami dining scene, my friend Jeff McInnis has recently opened his own restaurant, Root & Bone, in Brooklyn. Jeff's food is always special, his spicy fried chicken being no exception. With multiple layers of heat embedded in every step—even the sticky, pepper-infused lacquer announces itself with a fiery flourish—this bird is in a league of its own. Jeff is known for a masterful combination of tradition and originality, on display in a side dish of silky cauliflower mash that will make you forget potatoes ever existed.

BRINE THE CHICKEN: In a large pot, bring the sugar, salt, paprika, cayenne pepper, black pepper, and 5 cups water to a simmer over medium heat for 10 minutes, whisking to dissolve. Remove from the heat, add 5 cups ice water, refrigerate, and allow the liquid to chill to 40°F on a candy thermometer, 1 to 2 hours. Place the chicken in a large container and pour the cold brine over the chicken. Cover and refrigerate for 24 hours.

MAKE THE SMOKY SPICY PEPPER MIX: Combine the paprika, salt, and chili powder in a small bowl; reserve.

MAKE THE STICKY HOT SAUCE: In a medium saucepan, heat the oil over medium heat. Add the chiles and garlic and cook until just softened, 2 to 3 minutes. Add 1 cup water, bring to a boil, reduce the heat, and simmer until most of the water is evaporated, 13 to 15 minutes. Add the vinegar and cook over medium-high heat until the vinegar is reduced by half, 10 to 12 minutes (about 1 cup of liquid should remain in the saucepan). Using tongs, remove and discard the chiles and garlic. Add the cornstarch slurry and cook, whisking, until the sauce has thickened, about 30 seconds. Add the honey and salt and cook, stirring, until incorporated and slightly syrupy, 2 to 3 minutes. Remove from the heat and cool to room temperature.

5 cups all-purpose flour
2 tablespoons garlic powder
5 teaspoons onion powder
1 tablespoon paprika
1 tablespoon cayenne pepper
1½ teaspoons freshly ground
   black pepper
   Vegetable shortening, lard,
   or a combination, for frying

DREDGE THE CHICKEN: In a large bowl, whisk together the flour, garlic powder, onion powder, paprika, cayenne pepper, and black pepper. Remove the chicken from the brine, shake off the excess liquid, and dredge in the seasoned flour.

FRY THE CHICKEN: Fill a 12-inch cast-iron skillet halfway with shortening or lard and heat to 350°F. Place the larger breast pieces in, skin side down, along with the thighs. Fry, adjusting the heat to maintain a temperature of 325°F, until the underside is cooked, about 8 minutes. Flip and fry until cooked through and the thickest pieces reach 165°F on a meat thermometer, an additional 7 to 8 minutes. Remove from the skillet and drain on paper towels. Using the same procedure, fry the wings and drumsticks for 5 minutes, then flip and fry an additional 5 minutes. Drain briefly on a wire rack, then season with a pinch of the smoky spicy pepper mix.

TO SERVE: Immediately before serving, toss the chicken in the sticky hot sauce to coat. Serve with a generous helping of the cauliflower mash.

CAULIFLOWER MASH

SERVES 8

2 small heads cauliflower (about 4 pounds total),
   roughly chopped (about 8 cups)
2 cups whole milk
2 cups heavy cream
¼ cup (½ stick), plus 2 tablespoons unsalted butter
¼ cup cream cheese
3 sprigs fresh thyme
2 teaspoons kosher salt
   Chopped fresh chives and thyme, for garnish

In a large saucepan with a tight-fitting lid, place the cauliflower (reserving ½ cup) and the milk, cream, and ¼ cup butter. Bring to a low boil, then reduce the heat and cover. Let simmer, stirring occasionally, until the cauliflower is tender, 13 to 15 minutes. Add the cream cheese and thyme, then cover the saucepan and simmer until the cauliflower can easily be broken apart with a fork, an additional 4 to 5 minutes. Drain the excess liquid, reserving ½ cup liquid on the side.

Break the reserved ½ cup cauliflower into bite-size pieces. Melt the remaining 2 tablespoons butter in a very hot cast-iron skillet over medium-high heat. Add the cauliflower pieces all at once, and cook, stirring occasionally, until the edges are charred and blistered, about 3 minutes. Season with salt and pepper and set aside.

Using an immersion blender, puree the cooked cauliflower until smooth, or cool for 10 minutes and then transfer to a blender and carefully purée until smooth, adding the reserved cooking liquid to loosen if necessary (be careful to leave an opening for steam to emerge).

Transfer the pureed cauliflower to a bowl and garnish with the charred cauliflower, chives, and thyme.

PACIFIC RIM FLAVORS

WITH AN AGE-OLD EXPERTISE in frying and a passion for crispy food, Asian culture rivals its American counterpart when it comes to fried chicken obsession. In Japan, fried foods—crunchy, panko-crusted tempura and tonkatsu, as well as soy-lacquered chicken wings—are beloved favorites. So are dredged, battered, and fried boneless cuts of chicken, found in bento boxes all over the country. The same can be true of the fried birds of China, Vietnam, and Korea, where some of the most popular fried chicken today hails from. Some of the recipes here—such as Ma'ono's deeply crunchy, umami-packed interpretation (page 200) and Charles Phan's New Orleans–inspired chicken with Sriracha (page 197)—incorporate Southern-style elements with Asian touches, which isn't as much of a stretch as one might think once you consider, for instance, that Louisiana has one of the largest Vietnamese populations outside Vietnam. Others, like Ed Schoenfeld's General Tso's chicken (page 213), are faithfully authentic renditions of the original. From Korean-inspired fried chicken, with its light, crispy coating, to dishes prepared with flavor beacons of the Pacific Rim—sesame, Sriracha, soy—this group is all about heat, sauce, or crunch at any cost.

OPPOSITE: EN Japanese Brasserie Crispy Chicken, see page 198 for recipe.

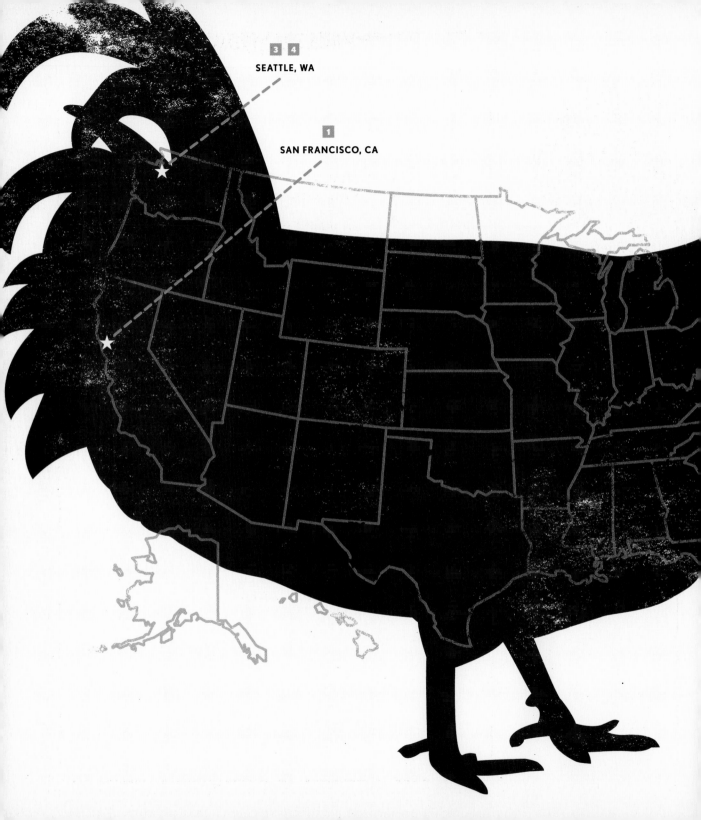

3 4
SEATTLE, WA

1
SAN FRANCISCO, CA

2 **5** **8**
NEW YORK, NY

6
BROOKLYN, NY

7
MIAMI, FL

HARD WATER'S FRIED CHICKEN

SERVES 4

FOR AIR-CHILLING THE CHICKEN

- 1 whole chicken (3 pounds maximum), cut into 8 pieces and patted dry
- 1 tablespoon kosher salt
- 2 teaspoons garlic powder

FOR THE SRIRACHA BUTTER

- 1 cup (2 sticks) unsalted butter
- 1 cup Sriracha sauce
  Juice of 1 lime (about 2½ tablespoons)
- 1 teaspoon kosher salt
- ½ teaspoon sugar

FOR THE DREDGE

- 1 cup all-purpose flour
- 2 teaspoons cayenne pepper
- 2 teaspoons kosher salt
- 1 teaspoon ground turmeric
- ½ teaspoon ground coriander

- 3 quarts canola or peanut oil, for frying

As one of our nation's most influential Vietnamese chefs, Charles Phan surprised the San Francisco food scene when in 2013 he opened Hard Water, a New Orleans–themed whisky bar, where he serves this incredible fried chicken. Inspired by a technique from his native country, Phan dry-brines his chicken before air-chilling it, uncovered, for 24 hours, which contributes to the extra-crispy skin (if you're in a hurry, even 12 hours makes a big difference). Hints of turmeric and coriander assert the provenance of Phan's inspiration, and the irresistible Sriracha butter will become your go-to condiment.

SEASON THE CHICKEN: Season the chicken with the salt and garlic powder and arrange, skin side up, on a baking sheet, leaving space between pieces if possible. Refrigerate, uncovered, for 24 hours. Remove the chicken from the refrigerator and allow the chicken to come to room temperature.

MAKE THE SRIRACHA BUTTER: In a small saucepan, melt the butter over low heat. Place the Sriracha sauce, lime juice, salt, and sugar in a blender or food processor. Blend on high for 1 minute, adding the melted butter in a slow stream to create an airy, emulsified sauce. The sauce will keep in an airtight container refrigerated for up to 1 month.

DREDGE THE CHICKEN: In a large bowl, whisk together the flour, cayenne pepper, salt, turmeric, and coriander. Fill a 6-quart pot halfway with the oil and heat to 340°F. Dredge the chicken in the flour mixture, shaking off the excess, and place it on a clean baking sheet. Set a rack atop a rimmed baking sheet and set aside.

FRY THE CHICKEN: Working in batches, fry the chicken, turning occasionally, until evenly browned and the internal temperature reaches 165°F, 12 to 14 minutes. Drain the chicken pieces on the rack; serve hot or at room temperature, drizzled with the Sriracha butter.

CRISPY CHICKEN

SERVES 6

FOR THE MARINADE

- ¼ cup potato starch
- 1 large egg
- 2 teaspoons soy sauce
- 2 garlic cloves, finely minced
- ½ teaspoon sea salt
- 2½ pounds boneless, skinless chicken thighs, cut into 2-inch-wide strips

  Sunflower oil, for frying

FOR THE DREDGE

- 1½ cups all-purpose flour
- 1½ teaspoons seasoned salt, such as Jane's Crazy Mixed-Up Salt
  Lemon wedges, for serving

We found the ultimate take on extra-light, extra-crispy Japanese fried chicken at New York's EN Japanese Brasserie, where the chefs marinate boneless, skinless thigh meat in a compound of soy, garlic, egg, and potato starch. The marinade serves double duty as a sort of edible glue that helps the seasoned-flour dredge adhere to the meat with ease. EN uses Jane's Crazy Mixed-Up Salt, but any seasoned salt that's loaded with dried herbs will do.

MAKE THE MARINADE: In a large bowl, whisk together the potato starch, egg, soy sauce, garlic, and sea salt. Add the chicken, toss to coat, cover, and refrigerate overnight or up to 24 hours.

DREDGE AND FRY THE CHICKEN: Fill a large pot halfway with oil and heat to 325°F. In a large bowl, whisk together the flour and seasoned salt until well combined. Working in batches, dredge the marinated thighs in the flour and fry at 300°F until crisp and golden, about 5 minutes for each piece. Drain the pieces on a wire rack and serve with lemon wedges to squeeze over the top.

NATHAN MYHRVOLD

CRISPY CHICKEN WINGS *and* SAUCE,
Korean Style

SERVES 4 TO 6

FOR THE SAUCE

½ cup gochujang (Korean fermented chile paste)
⅓ cup sugar
5 teaspoons soy sauce
2 tablespoons Shaoxing wine or dry sherry
1½ tablespoons toasted sesame oil
1 tablespoon minced fresh garlic
1 tablespoon minced fresh ginger

FOR THE WINGS

½ cup peanut oil
⅓ cup michiu (light) rice wine, dry sake, or dry white wine (do not use Mirin)
3½ teaspoons soy sauce
1½ teaspoons kosher salt
1 teaspoon toasted sesame oil
1 teaspoon MSG
½ teaspoon sugar
2 pounds skin-on chicken wings
Frying oil of your choice
¼ cup Wondra flour
¼ cup potato starch

He may have codified the exacting, science-heavy molecular cooking movement in an epic six-volume tome—2011's Modernist Cuisine—*but Nathan Myhrvold loves a plate of simply saucy chicken wings as much as the next guy. Inspired by a mix of Chinese, Japanese, and Korean flavors and techniques, Myhrvold briefly marinates his wings and coats them in a combination of potato starch and low-moisture Wondra flour before frying them to a perma-crunch—even after the wings drink up the accompanying sauce. The gochujang (a funky fermented chile paste), MSG, Shaoxing wine, and rice wine can be found at Asian grocers or online.*

MAKE THE SAUCE: In a small bowl, whisk together the gochujang, sugar, soy sauce, wine, sesame oil, garlic, and ginger. Cover and reserve at room temperature.

PREPARE THE WINGS: In a bowl, whisk together the peanut oil, wine, soy sauce, salt, sesame oil, MSG, and sugar until dissolved. Add the wings and toss to coat; cover and refrigerate for 30 minutes.

FRY THE WINGS: Fill a 6-quart pot halfway with oil and heat to 350°F. In a small bowl, combine the Wondra flour and potato starch. Sprinkle the flour mixture over the wings and toss to coat. Working in batches, fry the wings until golden brown, 6 to 7 minutes. Drain on paper towels, transfer to a bowl, drizzle with the wing sauce, and toss to coat. Serve hot.

MA'ONO'S HAWAIIAN FRIED CHICKEN
and Sesame Roasted Carrots with Tamarind Goat's-Milk Yogurt

SERVES 4

FOR THE BRINE

- 1 cup kosher salt
- 1 whole chicken, cut into 10 pieces
- 4 cups buttermilk

FOR THE MA'ONO SEASONING

- 1 ounce dried kombu (sea kelp)
- ½ ounce dried shiitake mushrooms
- 3 tablespoons fine sea salt
- ⅛ ounce (1 cup) bonito flakes
- 2 tablespoons soy sauce powder
  Pinch of freshly ground black pepper
  Pinch of citric acid (optional)

FOR THE DREDGE

- 2 cups all-purpose flour
- 1 tablespoon fine sea salt
- 1 tablespoon freshly ground black pepper
- 1 tablespoon onion powder
- 1 tablespoon garlic powder
- 1½ teaspoons soy sauce powder

FOR THE BUTTERMILK DIP

- 2 cups buttermilk
- 2 large eggs
- 1 tablespoon baking soda
- 2 teaspoons baking powder

  Canola oil, for frying

Growing up in Seattle, Mark Fuller waited all year to visit his grandmother, Lillian, on the Hawaiian island of Kauai. To make the fried chicken that filled picnic baskets brought on daylong hikes, Lillian whipped up a dredge using umami-rific Johnny's Seasoning. Now that he's all grown up and the chef/owner of Ma'ono Fried Chicken & Whisky, Fuller takes a page from the Proustian playbook, adding soy sauce powder to several elements of a densely crispy, mahogany-brown chicken that literally makes mouths water. At the restaurant he serves the chicken with roasted carrots and a tamarind-accented yogurt you may have to stop yourself from eating all by itself.

BRINE THE CHICKEN: In a large bowl, whisk the salt with 4 cups warm water until dissolved, then add 4 cups ice. Add the chicken, cover, and refrigerate for 6 hours. Remove the chicken from the brine and soak in cold water for 1 hour, changing the water every 15 minutes. Drain the chicken and pat dry with paper towels. Return the pieces to the bowl, pour the buttermilk over the top, then cover the bowl with plastic wrap and refrigerate overnight.

MAKE THE SEASONING: Preheat the oven to 350°F. Place the kombu and shiitakes on a small roasting pan and toast in the oven until fragrant, 10 minutes; cool completely. Using a coffee or spice grinder, crush the kombu and shiitakes into a fine powder. Pass the powder through a fine-mesh strainer to remove any large pieces. Combine with the sea salt, bonito flakes, soy sauce powder, pepper, and citric acid (if using). (The leftover seasoning can be stored in an airtight container for up to 1 month.)

MAKE THE DREDGE AND BUTTERMILK DIP: In a large bowl, whisk together the flour, salt, pepper, onion powder, garlic powder, and soy sauce powder. In another large bowl, whisk together the buttermilk, eggs, baking soda, and baking powder.

DREDGE THE CHICKEN: Fill a large (at least 6-quart) pot halfway with oil and heat to 360°F. Set 2 racks over 2 rimmed baking sheets and set aside. Remove the chicken from the buttermilk and drain on one rack for 3 to 5 minutes. Dredge the chicken in the seasoned flour, shaking off as much excess flour as you can. Dip the chicken in the buttermilk dip, then in the seasoned flour again, resting again on the rack between batches to remove the excess.

FRY THE CHICKEN: Working in batches, place the chicken in the hot oil; reduce the heat until the oil reaches 300°F, gently moving the chicken around to ensure even frying. Fry until the legs and thighs reach an internal temperature of 180°F, about 11 to 12 minutes, and the breast meat reaches an internal temperature of 165°F, about 9 to 10 minutes. Transfer the chicken to the clean rack to cool for 15 to 20 minutes. Once the chicken is cooled, return to the fryer and fry until the skin is extra crispy, an additional 4 minutes. Season the fried chicken with the Ma'ono seasoning and serve.

NOTE: The soy sauce powder and citric acid can be purchased at www.firehouse pantrystore.com; the tamarind drinking vinegar can be purchased at www.pokpoksom .com; and the kombu, bonito, and dried mushrooms can be purchased at Asian markets and gourmet specialty stores.

SESAME ROASTED CARROTS WITH TAMARIND GOAT'S-MILK YOGURT

SERVES 4

1	cup goat's-milk yogurt (or good-quality plain whole-milk yogurt)
1½	tablespoons Pok Pok tamarind drinking vinegar, or 1½ teaspoons tamarind paste plus 1 tablespoon Champagne vinegar
1	tablespoon (packed) light brown sugar
½	teaspoon plus ⅛ teaspoon kosher salt
16	thin carrots (about 1¼ pounds), trimmed and scrubbed, a few fronds reserved in cold water for garnish
1	tablespoon toasted sesame oil
¼	teaspoon freshly ground black pepper

MAKE THE YOGURT: Pour the yogurt through a coffee filter into a large bowl, refrigerate, and allow the excess liquid to drain for at least 6 hours or up to 10 hours. Transfer the strained yogurt to a bowl and stir in the vinegar, sugar, and ⅛ teaspoon of the salt; refrigerate until ready to use.

ROAST THE CARROTS: Preheat the oven to 425°F; set a wire rack atop a rimmed baking sheet and set aside. Pierce each carrot a few times with the tip of a paring knife. In a bowl, toss the carrots with the oil, the remaining ½ teaspoon salt, and the pepper. Place the carrots on the wire rack. Roast the carrots until tender and caramelized, 35 to 40 minutes.

TO SERVE: Make a bed of the yogurt and nestle the carrots on top. Garnish with the reserved carrot fronds.

KICK-ASS BATTERLESS FRIED CHICKEN
and Purple Waffles

SERVES 4

FOR THE CHICKEN

- 8 large egg whites
- 1 tablespoon smoked paprika
- 1 tablespoon garlic powder
- 1 tablespoon onion powder
- 1 tablespoon kosher salt
- 2 teaspoons freshly ground black pepper
- 1 whole chicken, cut into 8 pieces (or 8 of your favorite chicken pieces)

  Peanut oil, for frying

FOR THE BAGOONG BUTTER

- 1 cup (2 sticks) unsalted butter, softened
- ¼ cup minced red anchovies (available at Filipino markets) or one 3.5-ounce jar oil-packed anchovies, drained and chopped
- 2 tablespoons finely chopped fresh cilantro

FOR THE MACAPUNO SYRUP

- ¾ cup palm sugar or (packed) light brown sugar
- ¾ cup (1½ sticks) unsalted butter, softened
- 1 cup coconut milk
- 1 cup shredded young coconut meat or 1 cup unsweetened dried flaked coconut, rehydrated for 30 minutes in boiling water and drained

At Maharlika, a relatively recent addition to the New York City dining scene, modern Filipino cuisine is being introduced to an appreciative and rapidly growing audience. When we heard they had an unusual chicken and waffles item on their weekend brunch menu, we raced over to try it. Marinated and fried in heavily spiced egg whites, the otherwise undressed chicken emerges with gorgeously gnarled, crispy skin—think of it as Korean fried chicken's hipper cousin. The waffle, made with ube (purple yam) extract, is a mind-blower, its blueberry-hued interior worthy of a Dr. Seuss story. If you can't find the extract, simply leave it out—the waffle will still be crisp-edged and mildly sweet. The tangy, anchovy-laced butter is inspired by a classic fermented Filipino condiment, and the rich syrup by a strain of coconut indigenous to the Philippines. Both create a pleasing cacophony of flavor, but if you're short on time, well-salted butter and good-quality maple syrup are worthy swap-ins.

MARINATE THE CHICKEN: In a blender or a large bowl, combine the egg whites, smoked paprika, garlic powder, onion powder, salt, and pepper until well incorporated and foamy. In a bowl or Ziploc bag, combine the chicken and the egg white mixture, seal or cover tightly, and refrigerate for 8 hours or overnight.

MAKE THE BAGOONG BUTTER: In the bowl of an electric mixer, blend the butter, anchovies, and cilantro using the paddle attachment. Transfer the butter to a pastry bag fitted with a fluted tip. Pipe inch-wide florets onto a sheet of wax paper and refrigerate. Once chilled, transfer to an airtight container and refrigerate.

MAKE THE MACAPUNO SYRUP: In a medium saucepan over low heat, melt the sugar, then cook until caramelized, 5 to 6 minutes. Add the butter and whisk in until melted, then whisk in the coconut milk. Remove from the heat and stir in the coconut meat. Cover and keep warm over low heat.

- ¼ cup (½ stick) unsalted butter
- 1 13.5-ounce can coconut milk
- ⅔ cup sugar
- ⅓ cup dehydrated ube (purple yam) powder
- 1 teaspoon vanilla extract

FOR THE WAFFLES

- ¼ cup (½ stick) unsalted butter, melted and cooled
- ⅓ cup vegetable oil
- 2 large eggs
- 2 teaspoons ube extract
- 2 cups all-purpose flour
- ⅓ cup sugar
- 4 teaspoons baking powder
- ½ teaspoon kosher salt
  Cooking spray, for the waffles

  Peanut oil, for frying

In the Philippines, purple *ube* yams are ubiquitous in ice cream, *halo-halo* (shaved ice dessert), and pastries. The waffle's *ube* extract provides both vibrant color and a subtle nuttiness, which is enhanced by the jam's *ube* powder. If you can't find *ube* extract, chef Miguel Trinidad suggests equal parts vanilla and pistachio extract.

MAKE THE UBE JAM: In a small saucepan, melt the butter over medium-low heat, then add the coconut milk, sugar, ube powder, and vanilla. Bring the liquid to a boil, then reduce the heat and simmer, stirring constantly, until the syrup has thickened, about 5 minutes.

MAKE THE WAFFLES: In a medium bowl, whisk together the butter, oil, eggs, ube extract, and about 1½ cups water until well combined. In a large bowl, whisk together the flour, sugar, baking powder, and salt. Add the wet ingredients to the dry, whisk until just incorporated, and then fold the ube jam into the batter. Heat the waffle iron on the highest setting. Using ½ cup of batter at a time, cook waffles until crisp, 4 to 5 minutes.

FRY THE CHICKEN: Fill a large (at least 6-quart) pot halfway with oil and heat to 350°F. Remove the chicken from the egg white mixture and fry until crispy and the chicken reaches an internal temperature of 160°F, 13 to 15 minutes. Drain on paper towels and let rest for 5 to 7 minutes before serving. Serve the chicken on top of the waffles, along with the macapuno syrup and the bagoong butter.

Maharlika's Kick-Ass Batterless Fried Chicken and Purple Waffles

DALE TALDE

KUNG PAO CHICKEN WINGS

SERVES 8-10

FOR THE SZECHUAN OIL

- 1½ tablespoons annatto seeds
- 1 piece star anise
- 2 tablespoons Szechuan peppercorns
- 1 cup canola oil

FOR THE KUNG PAO SAUCE

- 1 13-ounce jar *toban djan* (fermented chili bean sauce)
- 1 cup bottled oyster sauce
- ⅔ cup Shaoxing wine
- ⅔ cup rice vinegar
- ⅔ cup sweet chili sauce
- 3 tablespoons toasted sesame oil

FOR THE CHICKEN

- 3 cups rice flour
  Canola oil, for frying
- 4 pounds chicken wings
  Chopped peanuts, chopped cilantro, and sliced scallion greens, for garnish

When a chef gets a craving, nothing stands in the way of scratching that itch. One night at his eponymous Brooklyn restaurant, former Top Chef contestant Dale Talde tasked his cooks with replicating the Americanized version of kung pao that they all jones for after grueling double kitchen shifts. When nothing but a hit of salty, spicy, tangy goodness will do, this should be your go-to recipe. You can find the toban djan, annatto seeds, Szechuan peppercorns, and other ingredients at any well-stocked Asian market, or venture to an online source to fill out your pantry. A double fry may seem fussy, but the results—tender meat and a crunchy, sauce-soaked shell—make it oh-so-very worthwhile.

MAKE THE SZECHUAN OIL: Combine the annatto seeds, star anise, Szechuan peppercorns, and canola oil in a small saucepan. Gently bring the oil to a simmer, turn off the heat, and let the spices steep for 30 minutes. Strain the oil through a fine-mesh sieve into a small bowl, discarding any solids.

MAKE THE KUNG PAO SAUCE: In a medium bowl, whisk together the *toban djan*, oyster sauce, wine, vinegar, chili sauce, sesame oil, and the prepared Szechuan oil. Reserve.

FRY THE CHICKEN: In a large bowl, whisk together the rice flour and 2½ cups water to form a batter with the consistency of crepe batter, adding additional water by the tablespoonful if necessary. Fill a large pot halfway with oil and heat to 275°F. Working in batches, dredge the wings in the rice batter, shaking off the excess, and fry until lightly golden, about 10 minutes. Transfer to a rack and cool for 15 minutes.

Raise the oil temperature to 325°F and fry the wings in batches until golden brown and cooked through, an additional 6 to 7 minutes. Drain the wings of any excess oil, then transfer to a large bowl and toss in the kung pao sauce. Garnish with peanuts, cilantro, and scallions.

FRIED CHICKEN

SERVES 4

Canola oil, for frying

1 whole chicken, cut into quarters

1 cup best-quality chicken stock, preferably homemade or bought at a gourmet market

¼ cup soy sauce

¼ cup finely chopped jalapeño or serrano peppers, seeded if desired

½ cup chopped scallions (white and green parts)

Sometimes the best things really do come in small packages—this is certainly the case with the unbelievably tasty bird they fry up at Hy Vong, a tiny Vietnamese eatery in Miami's Little Havana neighborhood. Since they don't take reservations, I show up for a true "early bird" special, and end up eating what feels like a very late lunch. This recipe—pan-fried in a shallow slick of oil, so the chicken skin itself becomes its crispy exterior—is simple, fresh, and delicious, with just the right amount of spice. It's important to use very good chicken stock, which helps contribute to the depth and body of the relatively thin soy-laced sauce.

Heat 1 inch oil in a wok over medium-high heat. Add the chicken and pan-fry, without moving, until the bottom skin is golden and crisp, 8 to 10 minutes. Flip the pieces and cook on the other side, an additional 8 to 10 minutes.

While the chicken is cooking, make the sauce: In a small saucepan, bring the stock, soy sauce, and jalapeños to a simmer. Arrange the chicken on a platter, pour the sauce over the top, and garnish with scallions. Serve immediately.

GENERAL TSO'S CHICKEN *is a dish with a legendary pedigree. According to Chinese food expert and restaurateur Ed Schoenfeld, who co-owns the two Red Farm eateries in Manhattan, in pre-revolutionary China the best cooks were retained by wealthy patrons to prepare elaborate, multicourse banquets. Legend has it that a cook for the governor of Hunan province, General Zuo ("Tso") Zongtang, perfected the dish and named it after his boss. After the communist revolution, a cook from Zuo's household decamped to Taiwan, where he opened a restaurant featuring General Tso's chicken. The dish migrated stateside to two 1970s-era New York restaurants. As a young manager at one of them, Schoenfeld sampled General Tso's chicken dozens of times. While many renditions are sticky-sweet and heavily battered, Schoenfeld returns the dish to its Hunanese roots, with moist, juicy, triple-fried chunks of dark meat in a perfectly balanced, sweet-and-tart sauce. With each of the three fryings, the oil is heated to a slightly higher temperature, coaxing the chicken to a crisp on the outside while remaining tender within.*

ED SCHOENFELD

GENERAL TSO'S CHICKEN

SERVES 4

FOR THE MARINADE

- 1 large egg white
- 1½ tablespoons Shaoxing wine or dry sherry
- ¼ teaspoon salt
- ½ cup plus 3 tablespoons cornstarch
- 1 pound boneless, skinless chicken thighs, or thighs and legs, cut into 1½-inch chunks
- 1 tablespoon vegetable oil

- 5 cups vegetable oil, for frying

FOR THE SAUCE

- 2 tablespoons soy sauce
- 1 tablespoon dark soy sauce
- 1 tablespoon Shaoxing wine or dry sherry
- 2½ tablespoons sugar
- 1 tablespoon white vinegar
- 1 teaspoon *chinkiang* (black rice) rice vinegar or sherry vinegar (optional)
- 2½ teaspoons potato starch dissolved in 1 tablespoon water
- ½ teaspoon vegetable oil
- 5 dried red chiles, whole or broken (broken makes the dish very spicy)
- 3 garlic cloves, thinly sliced
- 1 teaspoon thinly sliced fresh ginger, cut into ⅓-inch squares
- 3 scallions (white and light green parts), cut into ⅓-inch pieces
- 1 teaspoon toasted sesame oil

MARINATE THE CHICKEN: In a medium bowl, combine the egg white, wine, salt, and 3 tablespoons of the cornstarch. Add the chicken. Using your hands, toss to coat until the cornstarch has dissolved, then add the oil. Cover and marinate the chicken in the refrigerator for at least 8 hours or up to 48 hours (the longer you marinate, the smoother the chicken will be).

TRIPLE-FRY THE CHICKEN: In a wok, heat the oil to 300°F. Place the remaining ½ cup cornstarch in a bowl, then add the marinated chicken, turning to coat evenly. Transfer the coated pieces to a colander, shaking to remove any excess cornstarch. Working in 2 batches, carefully add the chicken to the oil and cook for 30 seconds, stirring gently to separate the pieces from one another, until the pieces have just turned color. Using a spider, remove the chicken from the oil and rest it in the colander. Heat the oil to 375°F. Return the chicken to the wok and cook, stirring gently, about 45 seconds. Remove the chicken from the oil and rest it in the colander; Reheat the oil to 400°F. Return the chicken to the wok and cook until it develops a light, golden crust, an additional 1½ to 2 minutes. Transfer to a colander or wok strainer to drain. Clean your wok completely.

DRESS THE CHICKEN: In a medium bowl, combine the soy sauce, dark soy sauce, wine, sugar, white vinegar, rice vinegar (if using), potato starch slurry, and ½ teaspoon water. Place the wok over the highest possible heat, then add the vegetable oil and chiles (make sure to do this in a well-ventilated place—the smoke from the chiles can be quite caustic). Stir the chiles in the oil until they start to scorch and turn mahogany brown, then quickly add the garlic, ginger, and scallions and cook, stirring, for 15 seconds (don't let anything brown). Add the reserved sauce to the wok, stirring. As soon as the sauce thickens and comes to a boil, return the chicken pieces to the wok, stir to coat, and cook for 30 seconds. Remove from the heat, sprinkle with the sesame oil, and serve immediately over cooked white rice.

SANDWICHES, WINGS, LI'L BITS, AND SPECIAL DIETS

ONE OF THE BEST THINGS about fried chicken is that it comes in all shapes, sizes, and varieties—and is open to endless permutations and variations. Cutlets pounded, breaded, and browned in a pan are popular around the world and here at home; wings crisped and sauced are practically irresistible when placed on the table; boneless cuts fried and worked into an inventive taco show the versatility of a chicken tender; sandwiches envelop the star element in a host of convenient and tasty vehicles and condiments. Even skin rescued from the scrap heap gets a chance to shine in recipes that render its fat—unleashing a shattering crunch. We've also included a vegetarian "chicken" recipe, a gluten-free variety that will win over even hardened skeptics, and an oven-baked version that aptly approximates its deep-fried counterpart. Whichever you choose, we think you'll agree that there are as many exciting ways to prepare and eat fried chicken·as there are days in the year.

OPPOSITE: Son of a Gun's Fried Chicken Sandwich, see page 224 for recipe.

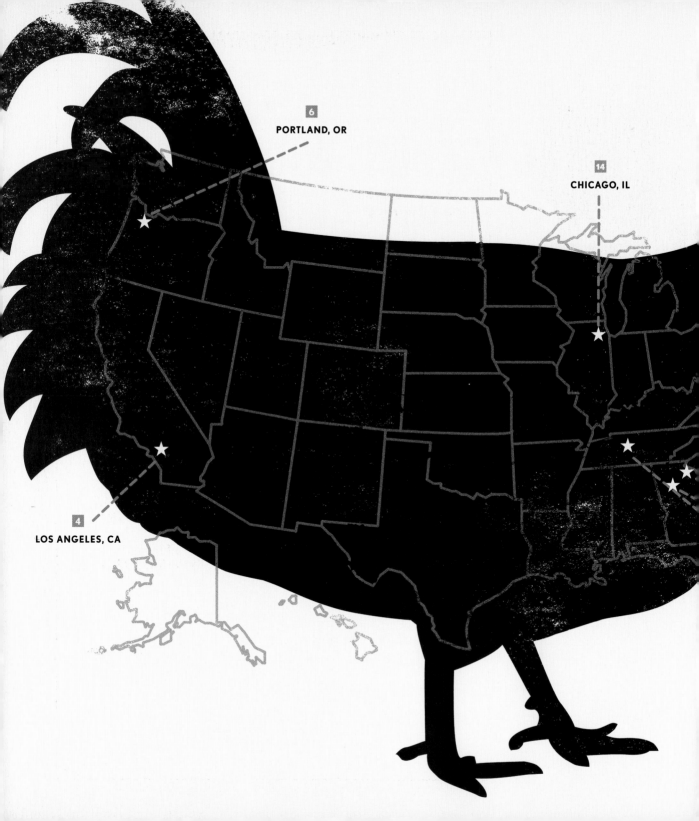

PORTLAND, OR 6

CHICAGO, IL 14

LOS ANGELES, CA 4

10
LONDON, UK

1
BUFFALO, NY

9 11 12
NEW YORK, NY

13
BROOKLYN, NY

5
CHARLESTON, SC

3
ATHENS, GA

2
ATLANTA, GA

5 7
NASHVILLE, TN

8
MIAMI, FL

1 *Buffalo Wings with Blue Cheese Dip*

2 THE ORIGINAL EL TACO
Fried Chicken Taco with Corn Elote

3 HUGH ACHESON
Fried Chicken Salad

4 SON OF A GUN
Fried Chicken Sandwich with Pickle Coleslaw and Red Rooster Aïoli

5 SEAN BROCK
Husk's Southern Fried Chicken Skins with Hot Sauce and Honey

6 KENNY & ZUKE'S
Gribenes Rillettes

7 KARL AND SARAH WORLEY
Biscuit Love Truck's East Nasty Biscuit Sandwich

8 VERSAILLES
Fried Chicken "Chicharrónes"

9 EDI & THE WOLF
Chicken Schnitzel and Dill-Cucumber Salad

10 YOTAM OTTOLENGHI
Seeded Chicken Schnitzel with Parsley-Caper Mayonnaise

11 ALEX RAIJ
Milanesa de Pollo à la Napolitana

12 ELLIE KRIEGER
Oven-Fried Chicken

13 CHEF RANDY REPPEL
Sweet Chick Vegetarian Fried Chicken and Waffles

14 INA PINKNEY
Gluten-Free Fried Chicken

BUFFALO WINGS WITH BLUE CHEESE DIP

SERVES 6-8

FOR THE BLUE CHEESE DIP

¾ cup sour cream
½ cup crumbled blue cheese
1 tablespoon whole milk or buttermilk
¼ teaspoon kosher salt
¼ teaspoon freshly ground black pepper

FOR THE WINGS

Peanut oil, for frying
30 chicken wings (about 3 pounds), wing tips removed, cut into 2 parts and patted dry
½ cup (1 stick) unsalted butter
¾ cup Frank's Red Hot Original Cayenne Pepper Sauce
Celery sticks, for serving

Up in Buffalo, New York, the Anchor Bar's wings are the stuff of legend. Ever since they were invented in 1964 for a group of hungry late-night patrons, many have attempted to duplicate the wings' well-guarded original recipe: deep-fried, then coated in a buttery-spicy sauce that must, and we mean must, be made with Frank's Red Hot Original Cayenne Pepper Sauce. Blue cheese dressing and celery sticks complete the picture. Current Anchor Bar owner Ivano Toscani almost laughed us off the phone when we attempted to extract his exact formula, but he practically challenged us to create the best replica we could. Ivano, here you go.

MAKE THE DIP: In a small bowl, whisk together the sour cream, blue cheese, milk, salt, and pepper. Cover and chill while you make the wings.

MAKE THE WINGS: Preheat the oven to 250°F. Fill a large pot halfway with oil and heat to 350°F. Set a wire rack over a baking sheet and set aside. Working in 3 or 4 batches, fry the wings until golden and crispy, 12 to 13 minutes. Drain the wings on the rack, then cover them with foil and place in the oven to keep warm.

TO SERVE: In a large pot, melt the butter over medium heat. When the butter is fully melted, whisk in the hot sauce until warmed through, about 1 minute. Remove the wings from the oven, add them to the sauce, and gently toss until fully coated. Serve with the blue cheese dip and celery sticks.

FRIED CHICKEN TACO *with* CORN ELOTE

SERVES 8

FOR THE MARINADE

- 5 scallions (white and green parts), roughly chopped
- 2 garlic cloves
- 1 teaspoon kosher salt
- ½ teaspoon ground cumin
- 2 tablespoons cider vinegar
- ½ cup corn or vegetable oil
- 1 cup buttermilk
- 8 2-ounce chicken tenders (or 1 pound boneless, skinless chicken breast, cut into 8 equal-sized strips)

FOR THE CORN ELOTE

- 8 ears yellow corn, shucked
- ½ cup mayonnaise
- 2 tablespoons lime juice
- 1 tablespoon hot sauce
- ½ teaspoon kosher salt
- ½ teaspoon sugar
- ¼ teaspoon garlic powder
- ¼ teaspoon freshly ground black pepper
- ¼ cup grated cotija (or Parmigiano-Reggiano) cheese, plus more for garnish
- 3 tablespoons chopped fresh cilantro, plus more for garnish

FOR FRYING AND SERVING THE TACOS

- 2 cups all-purpose flour
- ½ teaspoon kosher salt
- ¼ teaspoon freshly ground black pepper
  Vegetable oil, for frying
- 8 6-inch flour tortillas
  Lime wedges, for garnish

Atlanta's El Taco is the place to go for Mexican street food with a twist and this taco, starring an herb-marinated chicken tender, lives up to the hype. The corn condiment is inspired by the charred, spice- and cheese-dusted corn on the cob you'll find on virtually every street corner in Mexico. The combination of the crunchy chicken and the sweet, smoky salad—all folded into a soft tortilla—is addictive.

MARINATE THE CHICKEN: In a food processor, purée the scallions, garlic, salt, cumin, vinegar, and 3 tablespoons water until smooth. With the motor running, drizzle in the oil very slowly until the mixture resembles a thin mayonnaise. Transfer to a large bowl and whisk in the buttermilk. Place the chicken tenders in the buttermilk mixture, toss to coat, cover, and refrigerate for 24 hours.

MAKE THE CORN ELOTE: Heat a grill or cast-iron skillet over high heat and cook the corn, turning occasionally, until very slightly charred and just cooked, 7 to 8 minutes total. Cool slightly, then cut the kernels off the cobs into a separate bowl. (You will have about 5 cups corn kernels; discard the cobs.) In a large bowl, whisk together the mayonnaise, lime juice, hot sauce, salt, sugar, garlic powder, and pepper until smooth. Gently fold in the corn kernels, cheese, and cilantro until just combined.

FRY THE CHICKEN: Prepare a deep-fryer or a large (at least 6-quart) pot filled about halfway with oil to 325°F. In a large bowl, combine the flour, salt, and pepper. Dredge the chicken tenders in the flour two at a time, tossing well until completely coated; shake off the excess. Working in batches, fry the tenders until the chicken is golden on the outside and fully cooked through, about 7 minutes.

ASSEMBLE THE TACOS: Warm the tortillas on the grill, grill pan, or cast-iron skillet. Add one fried chicken tender for each taco, and top with about ¼ cup of the corn elote. Serve the extra elote alongside the tacos. Garnish with additional lime, cheese, and cilantro.

FRIED CHICKEN SALAD

SERVES 4

FOR THE BRINE

2½ tablespoons kosher salt
1 tablespoon maple syrup
1 sprig fresh thyme
6 black peppercorns
1 teaspoon mustard seeds
4 boneless, skin-on chicken thighs

FOR THE DREDGE

1¼ cups all-purpose flour
¾ cup cornstarch
½ teaspoon kosher salt
¼ teaspoon freshly ground black pepper

3 quarts canola oil, for frying

FOR THE CHICKEN SALAD

½ cup mayonnaise
2 large shallots, minced (about ½ cup)
1 celery stalk, minced (about ⅓ cup)
1 teaspoon Dijon mustard
¼ cup chopped fresh mixed herbs, such as parsley, tarragon, and chives
1 teaspoon crushed red pepper flakes
1 to 2 tablespoons hot pepper vinegar or vinegar-based hot sauce, to taste
Kosher salt and freshly ground black pepper
Soft rolls, crisp lettuce, and dill pickles, for serving

If you've ever wondered what to do with leftover chicken—other than eating it cold straight out of the fridge—here's your answer. Georgia-based Hugh Acheson makes good use of every scrap in this exceptional chicken salad. Its mayonnaise-based dressing and celery crunch would satisfy even the most discriminating picnicker, but it's the crunchy bits of skin—serving as a textural counterpoint to the salad's general creaminess—that make this recipe extra special. Though Hugh's delicious dark-meat fried chicken serves as the base of his salad, feel free to chop up any next-day chicken—white or dark—you've got.

BRINE THE CHICKEN: In a small stockpot, combine 4 cups water with the salt, maple syrup, thyme, peppercorns, and mustard seeds and bring to a boil. Reduce the heat and simmer for 5 minutes. Remove from the heat and cool completely to room temperature. Place the chicken in a nonreactive container and pour the cooled brine over the chicken. Cover and refrigerate for at least 8 hours or up to 12 hours. Drain the chicken, discarding any solids, and pat dry with paper towels.

FRY THE CHICKEN: In a medium bowl, whisk together the flour, cornstarch, salt, and pepper. Dredge the chicken in the flour mixture, generously applying to ensure that the mixture sticks to the chicken. Prepare a deep-fryer or fill a 6-quart pot halfway with the oil and heat to 325°F. Set a wire rack on top of a rimmed baking sheet and set aside. Carefully drop the thighs into the oil and fry until crispy and cooked through, 8 to 9 minutes. Using tongs, transfer the chicken to the rack, cool to room temperature, and then refrigerate until cold, at least 2 hours.

MAKE THE SALAD: Chop the chicken into small pieces and reserve. In a large bowl, whisk together the mayonnaise, shallots, celery, mustard, herbs, red pepper flakes, and vinegar. Season with salt, pepper, and more vinegar to taste. Gently fold the chicken into the dressing until incorporated. Serve with rolls, lettuce, and pickles.

SON OF A GUN'S FRIED CHICKEN SANDWICH
with Pickle Coleslaw and Red Rooster Aïoli

SERVES 4

FOR THE BRINE

- ¼ cup kosher salt
- 2 tablespoons honey
- 6 bay leaves
- ¼ cup garlic cloves, unpeeled, smashed
- 1 tablespoon black peppercorns
- 5 sprigs fresh thyme
  Juice and zest of 1 lemon

- 4 boneless, skinless chicken breasts halves (4 to 6 ounces each)

FOR THE DREDGE

- 4 cups all-purpose flour
- 1 tablespoon black peppercorns, lightly toasted, cooled, and cracked
- 1 tablespoon kosher salt

FOR THE AÏOLI

- 1 cup mayonnaise
- ¼ teaspoon very finely minced garlic
- 4 teaspoons Red Rooster Hot Sauce, or other Louisiana-style hot sauce
- ⅛ teaspoon kosher salt

FOR FRYING AND ASSEMBLY

- Peanut oil, for frying
- 3 cups buttermilk
  Kosher salt and freshly ground black pepper

Having made a name for themselves with the pork-centric cooking at Animal in Los Angeles, chefs Jon Shook and Vinny Dotolo now show a little love to the other other white meat—also known as chicken—with this sandwich, which they serve at the second of their three restaurants, Son of a Gun. From the chicken's divine brine and practically topographical crust to the pickle-licious slaw and devilishly spicy mayo accompaniments, this chick may just be the best thing since—and in between—sliced bread. At Son of a Gun they make their own bread-and-butter pickles, but since there are so many other homemade elements, they let us get away with suggesting store-bought here.

BRINE THE CHICKEN: In a saucepan, combine all the brine ingredients with 4 cups water and bring to a boil. Remove from the heat, add 4 additional cups of water, and let chill completely. Transfer to a large bowl, add the chicken breasts, then cover and refrigerate for 24 hours.

MAKE THE DREDGE AND AÏOLI: In a small bowl, whisk together the flour, peppercorns, and salt. In another bowl, whisk together the mayonnaise, garlic, hot sauce, and salt and refrigerate until ready to use.

DREDGE THE CHICKEN: Remove the chicken from the brine, rinse, pat dry, and allow the chicken to come to room temperature for 30 minutes; discard the brine. Fill a 6-quart pot no more than halfway with oil and heat to 350°F. Set a wire rack on top of a rimmed baking sheet and set aside. Place the buttermilk in a large bowl. Toss the chicken in the dredge, dip in the buttermilk, then toss in the reserved dredge again.

½ cup jarred pickle juice

¼ cup white vinegar

¼ cup grapeseed oil

4 cups cabbage (green or red),
   thinly sliced

1 tablespoon chopped fresh
   flat-leaf parsley

2 jalapeño peppers, seeded and
   sliced into thin rounds

¼ cup shaved red onion

⅓ cup store-bought bread-and-butter
   pickles, plus more for serving

4 *pain de mie* or brioche buns
   Softened unsalted butter, for the rolls

FRY THE CHICKEN: Fry the chicken until golden and crisp, 5 to 6 minutes. Transfer to the rack, season liberally with salt and pepper, and let rest for at least 5 minutes.

MAKE THE SLAW: While the chicken is cooling, in a large bowl whisk together the pickle juice, vinegar, and oil. Add the cabbage, parsley, jalapeños, onion, and pickles, toss to incorporate, and allow to marinate for 5 minutes.

TO SERVE: Split the buns, toast them for 1 to 2 minutes until lightly browned, and butter generously, then spread the aïoli on both sides. Arrange one chicken piece on the bottom half of each bun, top with a generous amount of slaw and a few pickles, then top with the top half of the bun.

HUSK'S SOUTHERN FRIED CHICKEN SKINS
with Hot Sauce and Honey

SERVES 4

FOR BAKING THE SKINS

- 2 cups chicken skins (ask your butcher to save them for you, or remove from 2 small chickens)
- 2 cups buttermilk
- 1 teaspoon cayenne pepper
- ½ teaspoon kosher salt, plus more for seasoning

FOR FRYING THE SKINS

- Peanut oil, for frying
- 4 cups all-purpose flour
- 1 teaspoon garlic powder
- 1 teaspoon onion powder
- 1 teaspoon smoked paprika
- ½ teaspoon freshly ground black pepper
- Honey and hot sauce, for serving

A fateful trip down the supermarket aisle got chef Sean Brock thinking. "I saw rows and rows of skinless, boneless chicken breasts and wondered where all the chicken skins were," said Brock, one of the main players in the New Southern cuisine movement. Soon thereafter he asked his supplier to send the skins his way, and these wisps of crispy goodness were born. A gentle buttermilk bath tenderizes the chicken while leaving just enough of the skin's distinct flavor intact. The result is a crazy hybrid of potato chips, pork rinds, and fried chicken all rolled into one. "These are a guilty pleasure you only eat once in a while," said Brock, who serves them at his Husk restaurants in Charleston and Nashville. "But people really go crazy for them."

BAKE THE SKINS: Preheat the oven to 350°F. Using the back of a knife, scrape away all visible fat from the skins (save the fat for use in a future recipe). In a large bowl, combine the buttermilk, cayenne pepper, and salt. Add the scraped skins to the buttermilk and toss to coat. Transfer the skins and buttermilk to a 10 × 10-inch baking dish, cover with tin foil, and bake for 1 hour, until the skins have tenderized and rendered some additional fat.

FRY THE SKINS: Fill a 4-quart saucepan halfway with oil and heat to 350°F. Set a wire rack over a rimmed baking sheet and set aside. In a large bowl, whisk together the flour, garlic powder, onion powder, smoked paprika, and pepper. Remove the skins from the buttermilk and coat liberally in the flour mixture. Lower the skins into the oil and fry, stirring every minute or two to prevent sticking, 3 to 4 minutes. Drain on the rack, season with salt, and serve hot, family style, with a drizzle of honey and a splash of hot sauce.

THERE WAS A TIME A *generation or two ago when many Jewish-American homes had a jar of gribenes—crispy bits of chicken skin yielded through the rendering of schmaltz, or chicken fat—on the table. Stirred together with deeply caramelized onions, the whole mess was spread on rye bread or toast and sprinkled with salt for an indulgent snack. Portland, Oregon's Kenny & Zuke's is part of a new wave of artisanal Jewish delis intent on revamping the classics for a new generation. Its chef, Ken Gordon, created these slyly elegant, crunchy rillettes just for us, adding a hint of fresh thyme and piling the gribenes onto thin rye toasts—think of them as "Jewish cracklings." Chances are, if you give your local butcher a day's notice he'll save you the chicken skin—and sell it to you for a song.*

KEN GORDON

KENNY & ZUKE'S GRIBENES RILLETTES

SERVES 8 TO 10 AS AN APPETIZER

3 cups chicken skin and fat (from 2 large or 3 small chickens)

3 large onions (2 pounds), peeled and diced (6 cups)

1 tablespoon chopped fresh thyme

½ teaspoon sea salt

¼ teaspoon freshly ground black pepper, or to taste
Microgreens, for serving

24 very thin small slices of rye toast, or packaged rye bagel toasts

PREPARE THE CHICKEN FAT: Spread the chicken fat and skin on 2 parchment-lined baking sheets and freeze until mostly but not completely solid, 1 to 1½ hours; the skin will still have a little bit of give. Cut the skin and fat into ½-inch-wide strips, then cut the strips into ½-inch dice. Heat a large cast-iron skillet over medium-low heat, add the skin and fat, and cook, stirring occasionally, until the skin starts rendering its fat and has shrunk to about half of its original size, 14 to 15 minutes.

MAKE THE CRACKLINGS: Pour a scant ½ cup of the fat into a large, heavy skillet and add the onions to the new pan. For the first pan, turn the heat up to medium-high under the chicken skin and cook, stirring frequently, until all the fat renders out and the skin turns a deep golden brown, an additional 8 to 10 minutes but just enough to prevent the skin from burning. When the skin is uniformly brown, strain and reserve the rendered fat, and spread the cracklings on a baking sheet lined with paper towels.

COOK THE ONIONS: While the cracklings are rendering, continue to cook the onions over medium heat, stirring occasionally, until they're very soft, 10 to 12 minutes, then turn up the heat to medium-high and brown them until they're very well caramelized, but not burnt, an additional 7 to 8 minutes. Remove from the heat.

MAKE THE GRIBENES: Place about ½ cup of the rendered chicken fat in a large bowl. Cover and chill in the refrigerator until solidified, but still soft, about 2 hours. Add most of the cracklings and onions to the bowl, reserving ¼ cup of each for garnish (don't refrigerate these garnishes!). Add the thyme, salt, and pepper, and gently toss until well mixed. Portion out the fat spread into small ramekins, and chill until ready to serve.

TO SERVE: Spoon some of the reserved onions on the top of the ramekins, then sprinkle each with a teaspoon of cracklings. Serve with microgreens and rye toasts.

BISCUIT LOVE TRUCK'S EAST NASTY BISCUIT SANDWICH

SERVES 10

FOR THE BRINE

- 2 cups buttermilk
- 2 tablespoons kosher salt
- 2 tablespoons freshly ground black pepper
- 2 tablespoons smoked paprika
- 2 teaspoons garlic powder
- 2 teaspoons onion powder
- 10 boneless, skinless chicken thighs

FOR THE BISCUITS

- 1½ tablespoons rapid-rise dry yeast
- ¼ cup warm water
- 2 teaspoons sugar
- 2⅔ cups soft winter wheat flour, such as White Lily brand (see note), plus more for kneading
- 2 teaspoons baking powder
- ½ teaspoon baking soda
- 2 teaspoons kosher salt
- 1 cup buttermilk (full-fat, if available), or ½ cup buttermilk whisked with 2½ tablespoons heavy cream
- ⅓ cup melted butter, plus more for brushing biscuits

For the tallest biscuits, use a convection oven if possible and make sure your biscuit cutter is as sharp as possible; dull edges limit the dough's ability to puff when cooking.

Karl Worley's Twitter feed, which broadcasts the whereabouts of his roving Biscuit Love Truck on any given day, has turned him and his wife, Sarah—both culinary school graduates—into Nashville's Pied Pipers of fried chicken. Lines form early for the East Nasty, a wet-battered, shatteringly crisp boneless thigh rested atop a fluffy-flaky biscuit made with White Lily flour, a baking staple in Southern kitchens. The rich, sage-studded sausage gravy further confirms this sandwich as a new classic.

BRINE THE CHICKEN: In a large bowl or resealable container, combine the buttermilk, salt, pepper, smoked paprika, garlic powder, and onion powder. Add the chicken, cover, and refrigerate overnight or up to 24 hours.

MAKE THE BISCUITS: In a large bowl, combine the yeast, warm water, and 1 teaspoon of the sugar and allow the yeast to bloom for 30 minutes. Preheat the oven to 425°F. In another large bowl, whisk together the flour, baking powder, baking soda, salt, and the remaining 1 teaspoon sugar. Add the yeast mixture, buttermilk, and melted butter to the dry ingredients, and stir with your hands to just combine (the dough should be shaggy, sticky, and wet; add an extra 1 to 2 tablespoons flour if necessary). Cover the dough with a clean kitchen towel or plastic wrap and rest in a warm area for 30 minutes to rise; the risen dough will still be quite sticky.

BAKE THE BISCUITS: Place the dough on a heavily floured surface, cover with more flour, and roll out to a rectangle about ¾ inch thick. Cut out biscuits with a 3-inch biscuit cutter and place on a buttered baking sheet, nestled together to touch, and brush the tops with butter. Allow to rise, uncovered, for 15 minutes. Bake the risen biscuits until the tops are golden brown, 11 to 12 minutes. Remove from the oven and immediately brush the biscuits with more butter.

Peanut oil, for frying
1¼ cups all-purpose flour,
    plus 1 cup for dredging
1 large egg
1 teaspoon baking powder
1 teaspoon smoked paprika
1 teaspoon kosher salt
1 teaspoon freshly ground black
    pepper
1 teaspoon garlic powder
1 teaspoon onion powder

FOR THE GRAVY

1 pound pork sausage, casings
    removed
¼ cup all-purpose flour
2 cups whole milk
2 teaspoons chopped fresh sage,
    plus more for garnish
    Salt and freshly ground black
    pepper to taste

    Grated white Cheddar cheese,
    for serving

White Lily flour is a Southern
flour made from soft winter
wheat, and is the biscuit-baking
flour of choice for Southerners
and beyond. It can be found
online, but if you must soldier
on without, a 50/50 blend of
all-purpose flour and cake flour
works just fine.

FRY THE CHICKEN: Fill a large (at least 6-quart) pot halfway with oil and heat to 350°F. In a large bowl, whisk together the flour, egg, baking powder, smoked paprika, salt, pepper, garlic powder, onion powder, and 1½ cups water. Remove the chicken from the brine and pat the chicken dry with paper towels. Place the dredging flour in a separate bowl and dredge the chicken in the flour, shaking off the excess. Dip the chicken into the batter, shaking off the excess. Working in batches, fry the chicken in the hot oil, being careful not to overcrowd, until the exterior is golden and crusty and the internal temperature of the chicken reaches 165°F, 10 to 11 minutes.

MAKE THE GRAVY: In a 10-inch skillet, cook the sausage over medium-high heat, crumbling with a spoon, until the meat is no longer pink, 3 to 4 minutes. Add the flour and cook, stirring constantly until the flour is absorbed into the meat, 2 to 3 minutes. Add the milk and sage, bring to a boil, reduce the heat, and simmer until the liquid has thickened, 1 minute. Season with salt and pepper to taste.

TO SERVE: Slice the biscuits in half. Place one fried chicken thigh on an open-face biscuit, then top with ¼ cup sausage gravy, grated cheese, and fresh sage. Serve with the biscuit's top half on the side.

BISCUIT LOVE

THE East Nasty · Buttermilk Fried Chicken, $8
Housemade Sausage Gravy, Buttermilk Cheddar

THE Princess · Nashville's Own Hot Chicken, $8
Housemade Pickles & Mustard, Tru Bee Honey

THE Colfax · Hickory Smoked Pork in a Green $8
Chili Sauce with Buttermilk Cheddar

THE Wash Park · Local Beef Burger, Pimento $9
Cheese, Chow-Chow, Fried Egg

THE GA Peach · Biscuit, Peach Truck Peaches, $6
Sorghum Whipped Cream

Charleston Tea Plantation
Sweet Tea
$2

Bottled Water
$2

Biscuit Love Truck's biscuit sandwiches; the daily offerings

FRIED CHICKEN "CHICHARRÓNES"

SERVES 6

FOR THE MOJO MARINADE

Juice of 2 oranges (½ cup)
Juice of 4 limes (½ cup)
6 garlic cloves, minced
1 tablespoon kosher salt,
plus more for seasoning
½ teaspoon freshly ground black
pepper, plus more for seasoning
2 pounds bone-in, skin-on chicken
breasts and thighs, cut into
2-inch pieces

FOR THE DREDGE

1 cup all-purpose flour
1 teaspoon kosher salt
½ teaspoon freshly ground
black pepper

Peanut or vegetable oil, for frying

Though mojo marinade can
be store-bought, take the
time to make your own. If you
must purchase it, Quincoces
recommends La Lechonera
brand Mojo Criollo, available
at Latin markets.

In Miami's Little Havana neighborhood, one Cuban restaurant looms larger than the rest: Versailles. Come in the morning to watch armchair critics discuss the fate of Castro-controlled Cuba, or at 3 AM to take the edge off a night of clubbing; either way, a plate of authentic Latin soul food awaits. One of the restaurant's most popular dishes is these bone-in chicken tenders, marinated in garlic and citrus before double-frying to a dangerously dark and crispy state. Chicharrónes are traditionally made with pork, but Ana Quincoces—better known these days as a Real Housewife of Miami, but a longtime food lover and coauthor with Nicole Valls of the upcoming Versailles cookbook—tells us that home cooks have been making them with poultry for generations. Quincoces recommends boneless chicken tenders for a kid-friendly substitute.

MAKE THE MOJO MARINADE: Combine the orange juice, lime juice, garlic, salt, and pepper in a glass bowl or large resealable bag. Add the chicken, toss to coat, cover, and refrigerate for at least 4 hours or up to 12 hours. Remove the chicken from the marinade, pat dry, and season the chicken generously with salt and pepper.

BREAD AND FRY THE CHICKEN: In a shallow bowl, combine the flour, salt, and pepper. Roll the chicken pieces in the flour, arrange on a plate, and refrigerate for at least 1 hour or up to 4 hours. In a large heavy skillet, heat 1 inch oil over medium heat. Working in batches, add the chicken to the skillet and cook until very lightly golden, 2 to 3 minutes per side. Drain on paper towels and allow the chicken to come to room temperature for at least 20 minutes.

DOUBLE-FRY THE CHICKEN: When ready to serve, heat the oil over medium-high heat. Working in batches, fry the chicken again until deeply golden and almost caramelized, 1 to 2 minutes per side. Drain on paper towels and serve immediately.

EDI & THE WOLF'S CHICKEN SCHNITZEL
and Dill-Cucumber Salad

SERVES 4

FOR THE SALAD

1½ pounds English cucumbers, peeled and thinly sliced
2 teaspoons kosher salt
½ cup crème fraîche
2 tablespoons Champagne vinegar
⅓ cup chopped fresh dill
2 garlic cloves, minced

FOR THE CHICKEN

4 boneless, skinless chicken breast halves (1½ pounds total)
Kosher salt, for seasoning
½ cup all-purpose flour
3 large eggs, beaten
1 cup plain fine bread crumbs
Vegetable oil, for frying
4 tablespoons lingonberry jam

There's no more beloved Austrian dish than Wiener schnitzel, a thinly pounded cutlet breaded and pan-fried to crispy perfection. Viennese-born, New York–based chefs Wolfgang Ban and Eduard Frauneder, partners in several Austrian-inspired restaurants and bars, created a version using chicken rather than the expected veal or pork. They recommend pounding the chicken delicately using the flat side of a mallet to prevent tearing, and breading the chicken delicately to encourage the schnitzel to puff during frying. To counteract the richness of the dish, serve the schnitzel with sweet-tart lingonberry jam and their delicious dill-cucumber salad.

MAKE THE SALAD: In a large bowl, toss the cucumber slices with 1½ teaspoons of the salt and let rest for 1 hour. Drain and discard the liquid from the cucumber. In a separate bowl, whisk together the crème fraîche, vinegar, dill, garlic, and the remaining ½ teaspoon salt. Add the cucumber and toss to coat. Refrigerate until ready to serve.

MAKE THE CHICKEN: On a flat work surface, place the chicken between 2 sheets of plastic wrap. Pound each breast to about ⅓ inch thick and season generously with salt. Place the flour, eggs, and bread crumbs in three separate shallow dishes. Dip the chicken in the flour, then the eggs, then the bread crumbs, shaking off the excess between each step.

FRY THE CHICKEN: Fill a large skillet with ¼ inch oil, heat until very hot but not smoking, and fry the schnitzel until golden brown and puffed, 2 to 3 minutes per side. Drain on paper towels and season with additional salt if desired. Serve with lingonberry jam and the cucumber salad.

Edi & the Wolf's Chicken Schnitzel and Dill-Cucumber Salad

UNTIL THE RELEASE OF HIS

cookbook chronicling the foods of his native city, Jerusalem, many people had no idea that Yotam Ottolenghi—the cofounder of a series of modern Mediterranean London restaurants that bear his name—was from Israel. There, schnitzel started out as a kibbutz staple, with the veal of the rarefied European original replaced with more readily available—and much more economical—pounded turkey breast. Now, virtually all Israeli schnitzel is made from chicken; to this day nearly all home cooks either make it themselves; store a supermarket version in the freezer; or buy it from home-style restaurants, where the crispy fried cutlets are often stuffed into pita bread or a roll piled high with salads and condiments. The version Ottolenghi created just for us contains five types of crunchy seeds in a variety of colors and textures, lending the exterior a nutty, exotic crunch.

SEEDED CHICKEN SCHNITZEL
with Parsley-Caper Mayonnaise

SERVES 4 TO 6

FOR THE PARSLEY-CAPER MAYONNAISE

- 1 large egg yolk
- 1 tablespoon Dijon mustard
- 3 garlic cloves, crushed
- 1½ tablespoons freshly squeezed lemon juice
- ¾ cup sunflower oil
- ½ teaspoon sugar
- 2 cups loosely packed parsley leaves, chopped
- 1 tablespoon salt-packed capers

FOR THE SCHNITZEL

- 4 boneless, skinless chicken breast halves (about 1½ pounds total), each piece cut into 3 long strips
- ½ cup all-purpose flour
  Salt and freshly ground black pepper
- 1½ cups panko bread crumbs
- 3 tablespoons white sesame seeds
- 2 tablespoons black sesame seeds (or extra white sesame seeds, if black ones are not available)
- 2 tablespoons flax seeds
- 2 tablespoons sunflower seeds, roughly chopped
- 1½ tablespoons coriander seeds, roughly crushed
- 1 teaspoon ground turmeric
- ½ teaspoon cayenne pepper
- ¾ teaspoon kosher salt
- 2 large eggs, lightly beaten
- ⅓ cup sunflower oil, plus more if necessary

MAKE THE MAYONNAISE: Place the egg yolk, mustard, garlic, and lemon juice in the small bowl of a food processor. Process on high, then add the oil in a slow stream until all of the oil is fully incorporated and the mayonnaise is thick. Add the sugar, parsley, and capers and blend 5 more seconds to incorporate. Transfer to a bowl and refrigerate.

MAKE THE SCHNITZEL: Working one piece at a time, place the chicken pieces between 2 sheets of plastic wrap and gently flatten each piece with a rolling pin, until it is just under ½ inch thick (don't worry if the schnitzels aren't perfectly uniform). Line a baking sheet with parchment paper and set aside.

MAKE THE FLOUR AND PANKO DREDGES: In a medium bowl, whisk the flour with salt and black pepper. In a separate bowl, whisk together the panko, white and black sesame seeds, flax seeds, sunflower seeds, coriander seeds, turmeric, cayenne pepper, and salt. Dip each piece of chicken in the flour and gently shake off the excess. Dip the floured chicken in the beaten egg, and then press in the seed mixture on both sides to coat well. Store the breaded pieces on the lined baking sheet and repeat with the remaining chicken.

FRY THE CHICKEN: In a large skillet, heat the oil over medium heat. Working in batches, fry the chicken until golden brown, flipping once, 4 to 5 minutes total, adding additional oil to the skillet between batches if necessary. Drain the chicken on paper towels and serve hot with the parsley-caper mayonnaise on the side.

BEFORE RECONNECTING *Spanish tapas with their authentic roots at her New York restaurants,* Chef Alexandra Raij was a food-obsessed kid with Argentinian parents—and a particular fondness for Milanese de Pollo a la Napolitana, *a saucy breaded cutlet that is one of the many Italian-influenced dishes found in the Argentine kitchen. Raij calls this a "doped-up, Basque-tilting version" of her mom's original dish, which was Raij's annual birthday meal request as a child; now her own daughter, Maayan, is a fan as well. Raij's simple tomato sauce, rich in olive oil and finished with a pat of butter for good measure, yields leftovers perfect for dressing pasta. (In a pinch, any good-quality store-bought tomato sauce can be subbed in for homemade.) Good-quality Spanish anchovies and Italian ham lend a salty edge, and a blanket of melted cheese cloaks the dish in crowd-pleasing comfort.*

MILANESA DE POLLO A LA NAPOLITANA

SERVES 4

FOR THE TOMATE FRITO (MAKES 3 CUPS)

- 1 cup extra-virgin olive oil
- 2 medium Spanish onions (1 pound), minced (3 cups)
- 1 teaspoon sea salt
- 2 cups crushed canned tomatoes
- 2 teaspoons chopped fresh marjoram, or 1 teaspoon dried
- 2 teaspoons chopped fresh flat-leaf parsley
  Crushed red pepper flakes to taste
- 1 tablespoon unsalted butter

FOR THE CHICKEN

- 4 boneless, skinless chicken breast halves (about 1½ pounds)
- 4 large eggs
- 1 tablespoon chopped fresh flat-leaf parsley
- 1 large garlic clove, minced
- ¼ teaspoon freshly ground white pepper
- 1 cup all-purpose flour
- 4 cups panko bread crumbs, pulsed in a food processor for 1 minute until fine
  Kosher salt to taste
- ⅔ cup extra-virgin olive oil, plus more for drizzling
- 8 good-quality Spanish anchovies, such as Ortiz brand
- 4 thin slices Parma cotto, or other good-quality baked ham
- 4 slices Provolone cheese
- 2 tablespoons fresh chopped marjoram, or 1 tablespoon dried
- ¼ teaspoon crushed red pepper flakes

MAKE THE TOMATE FRITO: In a medium saucepan, heat the oil over medium-low heat. Add the onions and salt and cook, stirring often, until the onions are translucent and tender but not browned, 15 minutes. Raise the heat to medium, add the tomatoes, and simmer until slightly thickened, 10 to 12 minutes. Stir in the marjoram, parsley, red pepper flakes, and butter and simmer an additional 2 to 3 minutes. Cover and keep warm.

MAKE THE CHICKEN: Preheat the oven to 450°F. Arrange the chicken between 2 layers of plastic wrap. Using a mallet or empty, clean wine bottle, gently pound the chicken ⅓ inch thick. In a wide, shallow bowl, whisk together the eggs, parsley, garlic, and white pepper. Place the flour in another wide, shallow bowl and the panko in a third wide, shallow bowl. Season the chicken liberally with salt, then pass the chicken first through the flour, then through the egg mixture, then finally through the panko, shaking off the excess after each step. Arrange the chicken on a large plate or sheet tray.

FRY THE CHICKEN: In a large skillet, heat the oil over medium-high heat. Fry the breaded chicken 2 pieces at a time until lightly golden, about 2 minutes per side (the chicken will be slightly undercooked at this point).

FINISH THE CHICKEN: Arrange the chicken on a baking sheet and drizzle 2 to 3 tablespoons of the *tomate frito* over each cutlet. Save the leftover *tomate frito* for pasta or other uses. Arrange 2 anchovies over each cutlet, then top each cutlet with 1 slice ham and 1 slice Provolone. Sprinkle the chicken with the marjoram and red pepper flakes and drizzle with olive oil. Place the baking sheet in the oven and bake the chicken until the cheese is melted and the chicken is cooked through, 5 minutes. Remove from the oven and let the chicken rest 1 minute before serving.

OVEN-FRIED CHICKEN

SERVES 6

Olive oil cooking spray

½ sleeve (about 20) whole-grain or plain saltine crackers, processed into fine crumbs (about ½ cup)

2½ cups corn flakes, processed into fine crumbs (about ½ cup)

2 tablespoons sesame seeds

½ teaspoon cayenne pepper, or more to taste

¼ teaspoon garlic powder

2 large egg whites

1 cup plain nonfat yogurt

1 tablespoon Dijon mustard

½ teaspoon kosher salt

4 bone-in, skinless chicken breast halves and 4 bone-in, skinless chicken thighs (3 to 3½ pounds total), washed and patted dry

Once in a while, you may have a craving for the crispy juiciness of fried chicken . . . without any frying whatsoever. For just such occasions we suggest this oven-baked recipe courtesy of healthy lifestyle guru Ellie Krieger, whose recipes never sacrifice flavor for virtue. Using readily available supermarket staples—yogurt, corn flakes, saltines—she's created a dish that can hold its own among the big birds. Removing the skin from the chicken drastically reduces the fat and calories, but thanks to the crunchy, mildly spicy crust you'll never notice the difference.

PREPARE FOR BAKING: Preheat the oven to 375°F. Lightly coat a baking sheet with cooking spray.

DREDGE THE CHICKEN: In a shallow bowl, combine the cracker and cornflake crumbs, sesame seeds, cayenne pepper, and garlic powder. In a large bowl, combine the egg whites, yogurt, mustard, and salt. Add the chicken pieces and coat thoroughly with the yogurt mixture. Then, one at a time, dip the chicken pieces in the cracker mixture, packing the crumbs evenly onto the chicken.

BAKE THE CHICKEN: Arrange the chicken on the prepared baking sheet and spray the pieces lightly with the cooking spray. Bake until the juices run clear when the chicken is pierced with a knife, 45 to 50 minutes.

CHEF RANDY REPPEL

SWEET CHICK VEGETARIAN FRIED CHICKEN
and Waffles

SERVES 4 (2 WAFFLES PER PERSON)

FOR THE FRIED "CHICKEN"

Vegetable oil, for frying
4 cups all-purpose flour
¼ cup cornstarch
1½ teaspoons paprika
1½ teaspoons onion powder
1½ teaspoons garlic powder
1 teaspoon kosher salt,
  plus more for seasoning
¼ teaspoon cayenne pepper
2 cups buttermilk
2 pounds good-quality seitan, cut in
  large pieces and drained of liquid
  Freshly ground black pepper

FOR THE WAFFLES

2 cups all-purpose flour
1¾ teaspoons baking powder
1 teaspoon sea salt
1¾ cups whole milk, plus more if
  necessary
4 large eggs, separated
10 tablespoons unsalted butter, melted
  and slightly cooled, plus more for
  greasing
3 tablespoons sugar
  Maple syrup and butter, for serving

Seitan, a gluten-based protein
substitute, can be found at health
food stores and Asian markets.

Brooklyn is a hotbed of fried chicken reinvention, and Chef Randy Reppel's Sweet Chick restaurant is no exception. But it's the restaurant's vegetarian recipe that intrigued us the most. With a lusty crunch and tender interior, minus the chicken itself, it's everything we love about fried chicken. To make this vegan, almond milk or soy milk can sub for the buttermilk in the "chicken" and the milk in the waffles; coconut oil works wonderfully in lieu of butter, and ¾ cup flaxseed egg replacer for eggs.

PREPARE THE SEITAN: Fill a 12-inch skillet just under halfway with oil and heat to 350°F. In a large bowl, combine the flour, cornstarch, paprika, onion powder, garlic powder, salt, and cayenne pepper. Pour the buttermilk into a medium bowl. Pat the seitan dry with paper towels and, if possible, squeeze with your hands to eliminate any excess moisture. Tear the seitan into large, rustic shapes and season generously with salt and pepper.

FRY THE SEITAN: Dredge the seitan in the flour mixture and pat off the excess moisture. Dip in the buttermilk, shake off the excess, and dredge in the flour mixture again. Fry in batches until golden and crisp, 11 to 12 minutes.

PREPARE THE WAFFLES: Preheat the waffle maker according to manufacturer's instructions. In a bowl, whisk together the flour, baking powder, and salt. Add the milk, egg yolks, and melted butter and whisk until just combined (small lumps are okay).

MAKE THE WAFFLES: In a separate bowl, use an electric mixer to beat the egg whites until soft peaks form, 2 to 3 minutes. Add the sugar and whip to stiff peaks, an additional 1 to 2 minutes. Gently fold the whites into the batter. Brush the waffle maker with melted butter and cook the waffles until crisp and golden, 5 to 6 minutes.

TO SERVE: Serve seitan and waffles with maple syrup and butter.

GLUTEN-FREE FRIED CHICKEN

SERVES 4

Canola or grapeseed oil, for frying
5 large egg whites
1½ teaspoons salt
1 teaspoon garlic powder
½ teaspoon freshly ground
white pepper
3¼ cups white rice flour
¾ cup brown rice flour
1 cup sweet white sorghum flour
⅓ cup tapioca flour
⅓ cup potato starch
1 whole chicken (about 3½ pounds),
cut into 8 or 10 pieces

To store and reheat leftover fried chicken, freeze the chicken in a single layer in Ziploc bags (refrigerated chicken loses its crispness). Reheat from a frozen state in a 275°F oven until crisp.

As the self-styled "Breakfast Queen" of Chicago, Ina Pinkney had collected so many accolades for her famous fried chicken that she could have easily thrown in the towel. But when an employee implored her to come up with a gluten-free version, Pinkney rose to the challenge, testing and tweaking until she arrived at a formula she deemed worthy of restaurant royalty. The secret is a blend of gluten-free flours (all easily sourced at your local health food store) and a long, slow fry that helps the coating adhere to the chicken like a second skin. The finished product may be pale compared to traditionally crusted recipes, but its audible crunch will silence even the most skeptical.

PREPARE THE OIL AND DREDGE: Fill a heavy, deep pot just under halfway with oil and slowly heat to 275°F. Set a wire rack on top of a rimmed baking sheet and set aside. In a medium bowl, whisk together the egg whites, ¾ teaspoon of the salt, ½ teaspoon of the garlic powder, and ¼ teaspoon of the pepper. In a large bowl, whisk together the white and brown rice flours, sorghum flour, tapioca flour, potato starch, and the remaining ¾ teaspoon salt, ½ teaspoon garlic powder, and ¼ teaspoon pepper.

DREDGE THE CHICKEN: Working in batches and starting with the breast pieces, dredge the chicken pieces first in the flour mixture, then in the egg white mixture, then back into the flour mixture, pressing down and packing on the flour mixture on the second dredging.

FRY THE CHICKEN: Working in batches, gently lower the chicken into the oil, skin side down, making sure not to overcrowd the pot. (Do not move the chicken for the first 10 minutes of frying, so the coating can set properly.) Fry until the pieces are golden and crisp, 23 to 25 minutes for the breasts, 19 to 20 minutes for the legs and thighs, and 15 minutes for the wings, or until the internal temperature reaches 165°F.

MASTER FRYING CHART

RECIPE NAME	PAGE NUMBER	CHICKEN TYPE
ARNOLD'S COUNTRY KITCHEN Fried Chicken	38	whole
HATTIE B'S Hot Chicken	45	whole
TYLER FLORENCE Fried Chicken	48	whole
CHARLES GABRIEL Country Pan Fried Chicken	57	whole
THE LOVELESS CAFÉ Fried Chicken	60	whole
LINTON HOPKINS "Naked" Fried Chicken	67	whole
JACQUES LEONARDI Jacques-Imo's Fried Chicken	73	whole
DONALD LINK Sunday Night Fried Chicken	88	whole
KERMIT RUFFINS AND RAY BOOM BOOM Hard Fried Chicken	97	whole
ELIZABETH KARMEL Hill Country Buttermilk Fried Chicken	98	whole
THOMAS KELLER Buttermilk Fried Chicken	103	whole *(2 birds)*
VENESSA WILLIAMS Cajun Moon Funky Fried Chicken	107	whole
MARY MAC'S TEA ROOM Fried Chicken	110	whole
SCOTT PEACOCK Edna's Fried Chicken	119	whole
MIKE MOORE Seven Sows Fried Chicken with Egg and Giblet Gravy	123	whole
ART SMITH Fried Chicken	125	thighs & drumsticks
JACQUES PÉPIN Fried Chicken Southern-Style	128	whole
ANDREW CARMELLINI The Dutch's Fried Chicken	131	whole *(2 birds)*
PAULA DEEN Best Ever Southern Fried Chicken	134	whole
MARTHA LOU GADSDEN Martha Lou's Fried Chicken	135	whole
GAVIN KAYSEN Café Boulud Skinless Fried Chicken	140	whole
MICHELLE BERNSTEIN Michy's Fried Chicken	144	whole
BLACKBERRY FARM Sweet Tea–Brined Fried Chicken	147	thighs and legs
MICHAEL SOLOMONOV Federal Donuts Fried Chicken and Sauce	151	whole
WYLIE DUFRESNE Popeyes-Style Chicken Tenders	158	Breasts *(boneless, skinless)*
ASHA GOMEZ Keralan Fried Chicken	163	thighs *(boneless, skin-on)*
MARCUS SAMUELSSON Coconut Fried Chicken with Collards and Gravy	167	Thighs *(boneless, skinless)*

BRINE OR MARINATE?	WAIT TIME	SINGLE / DOUBLE	SKILLET / DEEP FRY?	SIDES
no	——	none	skillet	Chicken Livers , Braised Turnip Greens, Fried Green Tomatoes
yes	overnight or 24 hours	double	deep fry	——
yes	2 hours or overnight	double	deep fry	Velvety Mashed Potatoes
yes	overnight or 24 hours	single	skillet	Candied Yams
no	——	single	skillet	Hash Brown Casserole
yes	24 hours	single	deep fry	Old Fashioned Coleslaw
yes	overnight	single	deep fry	Smothered Cabbage
yes	min 1 hour	single	skillet	Lake Charles Dirty Rice
no	——	single	deep fry	Cheesy Garlic Grits, Candied Country Ham
yes	2 hours	double	skillet	New Orleans-Style Vegetarian Red Beans and Rice
no	——	single	deep fry	——
yes	12 hours	double	deep fry	
no	——	single	skillet	Tomato Pie
yes	16–24 hours	single	skillet	Classic Buttermilk Biscuits
yes	48 hours	single	deep fry	Macaroni and Cheese
yes	24–48 hours	double	skillet	Swiss Chard Salad with Pine Nuts and Lemon
yes	2 hours or overnight	single	skillet	Corn Bread Sticks
yes	13 hours	single	deep fry	——
no	——	single	skillet	——
yes	2–3 hours or overnight	single	deep fry	——
yes	36 hours	double	skillet	Baked Beans and Barbecue Sauce; Pickled Fresno Chiles
yes	24 hours	double	skillet	Watermelon Greek Salad
yes	48 hours	double	deep fry	——
yes	overnight	single	deep fry	——
yes	overnight	single	deep fry	Popeyes Buttermilk Biscuits
yes	24 hours	single	skillet	Low Country Cardamom Waffles, Spicy Maple Syrup
yes	2 hours	single	skillet	

RECIPE NAME	PAGE NUMBER	CHICKEN TYPE
HONEY'S KETTLE Home-style Smashed Garlic Fried Chicken	169	whole
MARK ROMANO Highland Kitchen's Fried (Chicken)	172	whole
MICHAEL ROMANO Graham Cracker–Crusted Chicken	175	whole
MARIO CARBONE & RICH TORRISI Parm's Fried Chicken Cacciatore	177	whole
RUSTY HAMLIN Louisiana Battered Fried Chicken	179	whole
PIERRE THIAM Senegalese Fried Chicken	180	whole
STEVEN SATTERFIELD Yogurt-Marinated Chicken Thighs, Charred Vegetables, and Sherry-Honey Glaze	183	thighs *(boneless, skin-on)*
TUJAGUE Chicken Bonne Femme	184	whole
JEFF MCINNIS Fried Chicken	188	whole *(2 birds)*
CHARLES PHAN Hard Water Fried Chicken	197	whole
EN JAPANESE BRASSERIE Crispy Chicken	198	thighs *(boneless, skinless)*
NATHAN MYHRVOLD Crispy Wings and Sauce, Korean-Style	199	wings
MA'ONO'S Hawaiian Fried Chicken	200	whole
MAHARLIKA'S Kick-Ass Batterless Fried Chicken	204	whole
DALE TALDE Kung Pao Chicken Wings	209	wings
HY VONG Fried Chicken	210	whole
ED SCHOENFELD General Tso's Chicken	213	thighs *(boneless, skinless)*
Buffalo Wings with Blue Cheese Dip	218	wings
EL TACO Fried Chicken Taco with Corn Elote	221	tenders
HUGH ACHESON Fried Chicken Salad	222	thighs *(boneless, skin-on)*
SON OF A GUN'S Fried Chicken Sandwich with Pickle Coleslaw and Red Rooster Aïoli	224	breasts *(boneless, skinless)*
SEAN BROCK Southern Fried Chicken Skins with Hot Sauce and Honey	226	chicken skins
KENNY & ZUKE'S Gribenes Rillettes	229	chicken skins
BISCUIT LOVE East Nasty Biscuit Sandwich	230	thighs *(boneless, skinless)*
VERSAILLES Fried Chicken "Chicharrónes"	234	thighs and breasts
EDI & THE WOLF'S Chicken Schnitzel	235	breasts *(boneless, skinless)*
YOTAM OTTOLENGHI Seeded Chicken Schnitzel with Parsley-Caper Mayonnaise	239	breasts *(boneless, skinless)*
ALEX RAIJ Milanese de Pollo à la Napolitana	241	breasts *(boneless, skinless)*
ELLIE KRIEGER Oven-Fried Chicken	242	breasts *(bone-in, skinless)*
INA PINKNEY Gluten-Free Fried Chicken	244	whole
RANDY REPPEL Sweet Chick Vegetarian Fried Chicken & Waffles	243	seitan

BRINE OR MARINATE?	WAIT TIME	SINGLE / DOUBLE	SKILLET / DEEP FRY?	SIDES
yes	2 hours or overnight	single	skillet	—
yes	48 hours	single	deep fry	(Frozen) Cocktail
yes	30 minutes	single	skillet	—
yes	24 hours	single	deep fry	—
yes	overnight or 24 hours	double	deep fry	—
yes	overnight	single	deep fry	—
yes	2-6 hours	single	deep fry	—
no	—	single	skillet	—
yes	24 hours	single	skillet	Cauliflower Mash
yes	24 hours	single	deep fry	—
yes	24 hours	single	deep fry	—
no	—	single	deep fry	—
yes	14-16 hours	double	deep fry	Sesame Roasted Carrots with Tamarind Goat's Milk Yogurt
yes	8 hours or overnight	none	deep fry	Purple Waffles
no	—	double	deep fry	—
no	—	none	skillet	—
yes	8-48 hours	single	deep fry	—
no	—	none	deep fry	—
yes	24 hours	single	deep fry	—
yes	8-12 hours	single	deep fry	—
yes	24 hours	double	deep fry	—
no	—	single	skillet	—
no	90 minutes	none	skillet	—
yes	overnight or 24 hours	double	deep fry	—
yes	4-12 hours	single	skillet	—
no	—	double	skillet	Dill-Cucumber Salad
no	—	double	skillet	—
no	—	double	skillet	—
no	—	single	oven	—
no	—	double	deep fry	—
no	—	double	skillet	—

ACKNOWLEDGMENTS

To all of the chefs, restaurateurs, home cooks, and other enthusiasts who contributed your precious recipes to our project—thank you for sharing.

To Michael Salvatore at Sysco, a true team player and friend whose advice, flexibility, and knowledge smoothed the way for us.

To our friend Tom Stone at Bell & Evans: Your pristine poultry inspired both our testing and photo shoot. Thank you for your generosity and support of our project.

To Michelle Minyard, for leaving no chef's door unopened in New Orleans so we could capture the essence of this great food city in a way most people never get to experience.

To Kim Severson for the peerless fried chicken recommendations in Atlanta; your direction was invaluable. Also to John T. Edge for your insights.

To Caryl Chinn, Jesse Goldstein, Amy Mehlbaum, Kay West, and Terry Zarikian, who each pointed us to can't-miss joints with recipes to match.

To the South Beach and New York Wine & Food Festival teams and special-events department at Southern Wine & Spirits back in the office, whose hard work and commitment allow me the privilege and time to work outside of the festivals.

To Wayne Chaplin, for allowing me the freedom to do what I love most, and for the privilege of working for you at Southern Wine & Spirits of America.

To our amazing photographer, Evan Sung: Your wisdom, aesthetic, and laser-sharp vision are only matched by your appetite for authenticity (and Nashville hot chicken). **Thanks also to assistant Eric Bissell.**

To Jessamyn Rodriguez, Sandra Vu, and the entire Hot Bread Kitchen team. Testing our recipes at your inspirational facility only enhanced our process. Also to Adeena's culinary assistants Katherine Martinelli, Farideh Sadeghin, and Anat Abramov Shimoni.

To Pam Krauss, who believed in this project and helped guide us through the process of making it, and for assuring me that it does get easier the second time around. **To Jessica Freeman-Slade,** who kept up with the breakneck pace of this book's publication without ever losing your breath. Also thanks to **Doris Cooper, Kate Tyler,** and **Maha Khalil** at Clarkson Potter.

To food stylist Suzanne Lenzer, her assistant, Ashley Schleeper, and props stylist Kira Corbin, who brought a fresh perspective, impeccable taste, and good cheer to this process.

To Adeena Sussman, who not only helped me write this book, making my ideas and vision a reality, but effortlessly managed the entire process from start to finish.

To CJ Tropp, for getting me to and keeping me in the right place at the right time, and for always making order out of chaos.

Finally and most importantly, to RR for your never ending love and support, and for allowing me to still eat fried chicken every so often.

INDEX

Grateful acknowledgment is made to the following for permission to reprint previously published material:

Alfred A. Knopf: "Southern Pan-Fried Chicken" and "Classic Buttermilk Biscuits" from *The Gift of Southern Cooking*, by Edna Lewis and Scott Peacock with David Nussbaum, copyright © 2003 by Edna Lewis and Scott Peacock. Reprinted by permission of Alfred A. Knopf, an imprint of the Knopf Doubleday Publishing Group, a division of Random House LLC. All rights reserved.

Andrews McMeel Publishing, LLC: "Fried Chicken" and "Tomato Pie" from *Mary Mac's Tea Room* by John Ferrell, copyright © 2010 by John Ferrell. Reprinted by permission of Andrews McMeel Publishing, LLC.

Artisan: "Buttermilk Fried Chicken" from *Ad Hoc at Home* by Thomas Keller, copyright © 2009 by Thomas Keller. Reprinted by permission of Artisan, a division of Workman Publishing Co., Inc., New York. All rights reserved.

Clarkson Potter: "Sweet Tea–Brined Fried Chicken" from *The Blackberry Farm Cookbook* by Sam Beall, copyright © 2009 by Sam Beall. "Fried Chicken and Velvety Mashed Potatoes" from *Tyler's Ultimate* by Tyler Florence, copyright © 2006 by Tyler Florence. "Sunday Night Fried Chicken and Lake Charles Dirty Rice" from *Real Cajun* by Donald Link with Paula Disbrowe, copyright © 2009 by Donald Link. Reprinted by permission of Clarkson Potter Publishers, an imprint of the Crown Publishing Group, a division of Random House LLC. All rights reserved.

Ellie Krieger: "Oven-Fried Chicken" from *The Food You Crave* (Taunton Press, 2008). Reprinted by permission of the author.

Simon & Schuster: "Best-Ever Fried Chicken" from *Paula Deen's Southern Cooking Bible* by Paula Deen with Melissa Clark, copyright © 2011 by Paula Deen. Reprinted by permission of Simon & Schuster Publishing Group. All rights reserved.